Faculty of Health & Social Care

KT-379-251

The Open University

K207 The Law and Social Work in Scotland

Block
Adult Care 4

Prepared for the course team by Jeremy Roche

Based on original material prepared for the course team
by Kathryn Cameron, Lesley-Anne Cull, Jeremy Roche,
Janice West and updates by Debbie Baillie

The Social Work Degree Programme

The Open University
Walton Hall, Milton Keynes
MK7 6AA

First published 2007

Copyright © 2007 The Open University

All rights reserved. No part of this publication may be reproduced, stored in a retrieval
system, transmitted or utilised in any form or by any means, electronic, mechanical,
photocopying, recording or otherwise, without written permission from the publisher
or a licence from the Copyright Licensing Agency Ltd. Details of such licences (for
reprographic reproduction) may be obtained from the Copyright Licensing Agency Ltd,
Saffron House, 6–10 Kirby Street, London EC1N 8TS; website www.cla.co.uk/.

Open University course materials may also be made available in electronic formats for
use by students of the University. All rights, including copyright and related rights and
database rights, in electronic course materials and their contents are owned by or
licensed to The Open University, or otherwise used by The Open University as
permitted by applicable law.

In using electronic course materials and their contents you agree that your use will be
solely for the purposes of following an Open University course of study or otherwise as
licensed by The Open University or its assigns.

Except as permitted above you undertake not to copy, store in any medium (including
electronic storage or use in a website), distribute, transmit or retransmit, broadcast,
modify or show in public such electronic materials in whole or in part without the prior
written consent of The Open University or in accordance with the Copyright, Designs
and Patents Act 1988.

Edited and designed by The Open University

Typeset in India by Alden Prepress Services, Chennai
Printed and bound in the United Kingdom by Cambrian Printers

Aberystwyth SY20 3TN
ISBN 978 0 7492 1942 0
1.1

The paper used in this publication contains pulp sourced from forests independently
certified to the Forest Stewardship Council (FSC) principles and criteria.
Chain of custody certification allows the pulp from these forests to be tracked to
the end use. (see www.fsc-uk.org).

Contents

Introduction

Aims

- To introduce the legal framework of community care.
- To identify the range of community care services and for whom they can be provided.
- To consider the roles and responsibilities of practitioners working with adults who need community care services.
- To explore the key issues and dilemmas facing practitioners, service users and carers in this field.
- To outline the legislation relating to service users and carers.
- To consider the issues associated with the abuse of vulnerable people and the ways in which their welfare can be safeguarded.

This block covers a wide range of issues that are central to modern social work practice. It considers the legal framework and practice issues raised in work with older people, those living with disability and people with mental health needs. The same core social work skills are required for effective and ethical practice in this area as in other fields and their exercise is just as demanding as that needed when working with children and families or in the criminal justice system.

This block explores the law in relation to community care. It is in four sections:

1   Care in the community
2   Older people
3   Disability
4   Mental health.

The first section in this block provides an overview of care in the community, the legislative framework of community care and the position of service users and carers. The next three sections discuss the needs and interests of particular groups of service users who could be described as vulnerable – albeit for different and at times overlapping reasons – and the role of the social work professional in assessing their needs and delivering services.

Of course vulnerability has a number of dimensions. Some people are vulnerable because they are chronically ill or have a life-threatening condition, while other people might be vulnerable because of the behaviour of others towards them; they might be being abused or neglected in some way or the subject of discriminatory practices and attitudes. In the former situation it is an aspect of the person's health that has rendered them vulnerable – indeed they might have had a lifetime of excellent health until very recently. An accident might have dramatically altered their lives. Many people in such circumstances might experience considerable difficulty in coping with such a radical change to their life situation – a transition that can be made more difficult by the behaviour of professionals and key social institutions. Other people might have made themselves vulnerable, for example by substance abuse. People do not, however, set out to make themselves vulnerable – on purpose so to speak – but as a result of their substance abuse find themselves in poor health or in need of specialist services. They will be in need of support and health and social care professionals will need to respond to their needs just as they would to the needs of other service users; being judgmental (as opposed to exercising professional judgment) is not part of ethical or value-based social work practice.

However, older people, people with disabilities and those with mental health needs are often vulnerable not solely because of their situation or condition but because of social exclusion, or abuse, or society's attitude towards them. The Protection of Vulnerable Groups (Scotland) Bill was introduced in the Scottish Parliament in September 2006 to ensure that people who should not be around children or vulnerable adults cannot access them through work.

Box 1   Protection of Vulnerable Groups (Scotland) Bill

The bill builds on existing legislation, particularly the Protection of Children (Scotland) Act of 2003 and Part V of the Police Act of 1997. It closes operational loopholes in the current vetting arrangements and addresses frustrations felt by users. A single executive agency will be formed to support the new vetting and barring scheme. It will bring together Disclosure Scotland, which will undertake the vetting function, and the Central Barring Unit, which will undertake the barring function.

The bill's main provisions affect vulnerable adults in the following ways:

- for the first time in Scotland, create a disqualified from working with vulnerable adults list
- extend the current disqualified from working with children list
- introduce continuous updating of the barred lists to alert employers if new information about an employee comes to light that may indicate that they have become unsuitable for working with vulnerable groups
- establish a Central Barring Unit to assess whether someone should be placed on one, or both, lists
- introduce individual statements of barred status – allowing private tutors, for example, to prove they are not disqualified from working with children.

(Scottish Executive, news release, 2006a)

It is not, however, just a question of people being vulnerable because others might cause them harm in some way or abuse them: it is not simply a protection issue. 'Ageism', for example, can operate to exclude and marginalise the experiences and views of older people (Bytheway, 1990). Research commissioned by Age Concern (2005) found that one in three respondents thought that the over 70s were viewed as 'incompetent and incapable'. The report stated:

> Our lives are defined by ageing: the ages at which we can learn to drive, vote, have sex, buy a house or retire, get a pension, travel by bus for free. More subtle are the implicit boundaries that curtail our lives: the 'safe' age to have children, the 'experience' needed to fill the boss's role, the physical strength needed for some jobs. Society is continually making

judgements about when you are old enough for something – and when you are too old. But if we allow ageism to flourish unchallenged it means that 'too old' can lead to discrimination.

(Age Concern, 2005, p. 2)

Age Concern (2005) reported that from age 55 onwards people were nearly twice as likely to have experienced age prejudice than any other form of discrimination and that almost 30 per cent of people believe there is more prejudice against the old than five years ago, and that this will continue to get worse.

It is not just older people who are negatively affected by discrimination and prejudice. The 'see me' anti-stigma campaign is run by an alliance of five Scottish mental health organisations: Highland Users Group (HUG), National Schizophrenia Fellowship (Scotland), Penumbra, Royal College of Psychiatrists (Scottish Division) and the Scottish Association for Mental Health (SAMH). In November 2006 a number of Lanarkshire-based organisations demonstrated their commitment to tackling the stigma experienced by people with mental health problems by taking part in a simultaneous 'see me' pledge signing.

> **Box 2   See me**
>
> By signing the 'see me' pledge, a large number of bodies joined the local initiative, which now involves over 50 Lanarkshire organisations. The initiative to challenge the stigma associated with mental ill-health aims to eliminate the discrimination experienced by those with mental health problems across Lanarkshire. With so many local employers making a stand, the signing had a particular focus on tackling workplace stigma and discrimination.
>
> ('see me', 2006)

The campaign director of 'see me', Linda Dunion, said:

The tremendous level of enthusiasm in Lanarkshire is invaluable in promoting anti-stigma messages. Fear of other people's reactions often prevents people who experience mental health problems from seeking help and support in the workplace, or from applying for jobs for which they are qualified. By reducing the stigma we will make it easier for everyone to speak more openly about mental health problems.

('see me', 2006)

A similar message was conveyed by Duncan Mackay, head of Social Work Development, North Lanarkshire Council:

Most people with mental health problems can and do recover and go on to lead fulfilling lives. However we know that negative attitudes can make people's problems worse and hinder recovery. It is essential that we collectively encourage openness and understanding around the issue and prevent discrimination of people in Lanarkshire with mental health problems.

('see me', 2006)

The report *See Me So Far* ('see me', 2005) confirms the importance of challenging stereotypical views and attitudes concerning people with mental health needs. 'Getting people to see beyond the stereotypes, to recognise that people with mental health problems are our family, friends, neighbours or colleagues, has been an important first step' ('see me', 2005, p. 4). Further as Linda Dunion observes:

> One of the greatest myths of mental ill health is that people do not recover, while the reality is that around three-quarters do get better and get on with their lives, even though some may continue to have periodic or ongoing symptoms.
>
> The fact is that any one of us can experience mental health problems, but some of us are more likely to and it is perhaps no surprise that it is the most disadvantaged who are most at risk. Risk factors for mental ill health include poverty, unemployment, poor housing, homelessness, bullying, racism, drug and alcohol problems, sexual abuse, domestic violence and being in prison.
>
> ('see me', 2005, p. 2)

The 'see me' survey found that 57 per cent of those who had experienced mental ill health had concealed the fact when applying for a job and 43 per cent had not gone ahead with a job application for fear of how their mental health history might be perceived. Thus, for people who experience mental health problems, the elimination of stigma is a prerequisite to achieving a good quality of life ('see me', 2005).

The issue of different kinds of vulnerability underpins much of the legislation in Scotland that is relevant to social work practice. In Scotland in the context of consultations on the Protection of Vulnerable Groups (Scotland) Bill the consultation document referred to the Scottish Law Commission's definition of vulnerability (at para. 22). This stated that:

> a vulnerable adult should be defined... as an adult aged (16 or over) who is unable to safeguard his or her personal welfare, property, or financial affairs, and is:
>
> in need of care and attention arising out of age or infirmity, or suffering from illness or mental disorder, or substantially handicapped by any disability.
>
> (Scottish Executive, 2002, para. 22)

Some people, as a result of their vulnerability, may need extra support if they are to avoid dependency and residential care. This requires both resources and good practice on the part of social workers. Issues are also raised here about the quality of care in residential homes. As you will see later in this block, the local authority and the Scottish Commission for the Regulation of Care (popularly known as the Care Commission) have specific powers and duties in relation to the standard of care in residential homes.

Professional social work practice has a key role in empowering vulnerable service users, respecting their rights and in countering discrimination and promoting social justice. Thus social work practice in this area must be alive to the key themes of this course such as anti-discriminatory practice and the practical and ethical need to respect the different ways of living in society today. There are grounds for concern regarding the delivery of services to all groups in the community. Recent research commissioned by the Scottish Executive found that minority ethnic groups have poorer access to community care services than others, although their needs are similar. The research concluded that person-centred mainstream services need to be offered to all on an equal basis to avoid stereotyping minority ethnic groups and excluding groups with distinctive cultures (MacDonald , 2004). In a similar vein the Age Concern research (2005) found that while people from Asian and African-Caribbean backgrounds were much more likely to identify ethnicity or race as the most common basis of prejudice against them they were also much more likely than whites to have experienced age-related discrimination.

As noted above the issue of disadvantaging social attitudes is not, however, confined to how society views older people. Those with learning difficulties or mental health needs also experience social exclusion and prejudice. The SAMH report (2006) *A World to Belong to* found that compared with the general public, people using mental health services had less social support. It found that when compared with the rest of society:

- people using mental health services were more than four times as likely to live alone
- they were more than twice as likely not to have a partner.

Shona Neil the chief executive of SAMH said:

> The next challenge is for the world in general to be more inclusive of people with mental health problems, and more willing to accept that the world belongs to all of us.
>
> (SAMH, 2006)

In this block you will consider the range of legislation relating to older people, people with physical and learning disabilities and people with severe mental health needs. Working with such service users and involving them and their families and communities in meeting their needs, is a highly skilled and demanding task. The approaches required when working with and supporting such service users are central to good social work practice. A commitment to empowering service users and treating them with respect at all times is as important in this area as it is in other fields of social work practice. Listening to what service users themselves have to say about their needs and how they might be met, and taking into account their carers' views, are also integral to good practice in this area.

1 Care in the community

For this section you need:

- audio CD
- course website access for online activities
- Reader, Chapter 11.

Core questions

- What are community care services?
- What is the legal framework of community care?
- What is the importance of assessment within the framework of care in the community?
- What are the key elements of care management?

Care in the community focuses on a better quality of life

1.1 Introduction

The White Paper Caring for People (Department of Health, 1989), with its emphasis on a 'mixed economy of care', marked a change in emphasis and approach in Scotland. While the SHARPEN Report (Scottish Home and Health Department/Scottish Health Service Planning Council,1988) had assumed a lead role for health services, the White Paper placed the lead role on social work departments. The White Paper's objectives for community care are set out in Box 3 – they are recognisably issues of continuing importance today.

Box 3   Caring for people

To enable people to live as normal a life as possible in their own homes or in a homely environment in the local community.

To provide the right amount of care and support to help people achieve maximum possible independence and, by acquiring or re-acquiring basic living skills, help them achieve their full potential.

To give people a greater individual say in how they live their lives and the service they need to help them to do so.

To promote the development of domiciliary, day and respite services to enable people to live in their own homes wherever feasible and sensible.

To ensure service providers make practical support for carers a high priority.

To make proper assessment of need and good case management the cornerstone of high quality care.

To promote the development of a flourishing independent sector alongside good quality public services.

To clarify the responsibilities of agencies and so make it easier to hold them to account for their performance.

To secure better value for taxpayers' money by introducing a new funding structure for social care.

In 1998 the Scottish Office published *Modernising Community Care* (1998a), which set out the following aims:

- quicker and better decision making, through delegated decision making and financial responsibility
- more flexible and better quality home care services, including a shift in the balance of care towards these services
- agencies working in partnership in localities, through better operational and strategic planning, joint budgets, joint services and joint systems.

Today the debates surrounding adult care centre not just on the issue of social justice and an end to discrimination, they also raise such issues as resource priorities and healthcare rationing, the delivery of free personal care, the quality of social care services and how best to empower service users and promote their independent living. At the centre of this is not only the question of state support for service users but also the form that that support should take. For example many older people (and their carers and relatives) want to remain in their own homes and want services to be arranged so as to make that possible. However, such services can be very expensive and some older people are in need of nursing care, which might only be available in residential care. The costs of supporting the health and social care needs of older people are also increasing.

According to Age Concern (2003):

- Around a third of a million Scots are over 75.
- One in five people in Scotland is aged over 60, life expectancy is increasing and the number of people over 80 will significantly increase over the next 20 years.
- 15 per cent of people over 70 years of age in Scotland have a disability and 17 per cent have a long-term illness.

The *Report of the 21st Century Social Work Review* points out that in 1968 18 per cent of the population was aged over 60 – by 2030 it will be 25 per cent with those over 75 increasing by 60 per cent by 2028 (Scottish Executive, 2006b, p. 18). People aged over 75 are most likely to have higher dependency and more complex health needs. However gender, ethnicity and socio-economic status have an impact on health and life expectancy. In 2003 Age Concern published a briefing paper that looked at a number of issues around health and older people. On the question of access the briefing paper observed that appropriate transport can be an issue as can lack of knowledge about what help is available and an inability to get referred to an appropriate service. Age Concern point out that older people experiencing ill health may feel vulnerable and find it difficult to negotiate the healthcare system; they need access to independent, good quality advocacy. The problem of access is exacerbated by the under-resourcing of community services that would help people to stay healthy and maintain their independence. It is also important to recognise that older people can have complex health needs that require a range of services: not just from the health sector.

Box 4   Age Concern health policy objectives

The key policy objectives for Age Concern Scotland (2003) are:

- to achieve fair access to health services, on the basis of clinical need, not age alone
- to reduce health inequalities affecting older people
- to change attitudes to ageing in healthcare and amongst health policymakers
- to challenge direct and indirect age discrimination in health policy and practice
- to promote a positive image of older people as a diverse group who can be healthy, active and independent
- to ensure that the healthcare system is shaped around older people's and carers' needs
- to promote older people's involvement in healthcare and health planning, delivery and evaluation
- to protect and increase older people's right to information, choice, dignity and respect in healthcare and health, ensuring that they have adequate means of redress if necessary
- to ensure that future health policy and the continued modernisation of healthcare considers the needs of older people
- to highlight areas where access to, and quality of, services that older people receive is not equal to other patient groups, and to ensure that suitable measures are developed to monitor this.

[Handwritten margin notes: "update. Age Scotland etc. (age uk to argue?) Keep in mind — influences for social work involvement"]

At the root of older people's continuing concern around adult care is the lack of respect they are shown and the undermining of their independence by health and social care professionals and the institutions they work for. Fundamentally their demand is that their experiences and perspectives are taken seriously – indeed this is the demand of all adult care service users. In this respect there is an interesting parallel with the children's rights movement with its emphasis on the recognition of interdependency and the importance of respecting the voices of children and young people. For all service users the current emphasis on partnership and consultation is very welcome, carrying as it does the key recognition that any commitment to promoting the welfare and well-being of vulnerable people irrespective of their age, ethnicity, religion and sexuality entails listening to what they have to say about their own condition and situation. This is not to say that the views of service users should always prevail – it is, however, critical as a professional to acknowledge the importance of their perspective and to genuinely take their views into account. Sometimes it will only be through working in partnership and fashioning new solutions that a practical way forward can be found that meets the needs of the service user.

Some issues have, however, become more important over recent years and one of these is the perceived need for improved joint working and information sharing. In 1999 the Scottish Executive established the Joint Future Group with a remit to find ways to improve joint working in order to deliver modern and effective person-centred services and to agree a list of joint measures that all local authorities, health boards and trusts should have in place to deliver effective services, and to set deadlines by which this must be done.

In November 2000 the Joint Future Group report was published setting out recommendations for improvements in community care (some of which have already been implemented) (Scottish Executive, 2000a). Key recommendations are summarised in Box 5.

Joint Working

Box 5   Joint Future Group Report

- Every local authority area should have in place a comprehensive, joint hospital discharge/rapid response team, by mid 2001–2002.
- Every local authority area should have in place a comprehensive, joint intensive home support team, by mid 2001–2002.
- Each year, agencies should provide both more short breaks (to reduce the number of carers providing most care, without a break), and more breaks at home.
- Every local authority should identify the need for a practical shopping/domestic/household service, and arrange it comprehensively, by mid 2001–2002.
- The Executive should, in 2001, set up an older people's service development centre to champion the development of good and innovative community care services, promote training and assist implementation of the Group's proposals.
- Agencies locally should have in place single, shared assessment procedures for older people and for those with dementia by October 2001, and for all client groups by April 2002.
- The Scottish Executive should redefine care management as 'Intensive Care Management', which will be for people with complex or frequently changing needs and care managers should be trained in 'Intensive Care Management' throughout 2001–2002. Only those who have undertaken such training should carry out 'Intensive Care Management'.
- The Scottish Executive should, by 2002, offer a strategic lead on the development of community care information, information sharing and systems integration.

Joint Working

- Local authorities (that is, social work and housing), health boards, NHS trusts and Scottish Homes should draw up local partnership agreements, including a clear programme for local joint resourcing and joint management of community care services collectively or for each care user group individually.
- As a step towards that, and recognising current progress on the ground, every area should introduce joint resourcing and joint management of services for older people from April 2002.
- The Convention of Scottish Local Authorities (COSLA) should develop guidance on charging policies to reduce the inconsistencies in home care charging.
- The Scottish Executive should consider introducing:
  - free home care for up to four weeks for older people leaving hospital
  - free home care for older people receiving 'extended home care' (though they would still pay for 'ordinary' services).

Good for TMA 2

The Scottish Executive immediately committed to the following:

- more intensive care at home;
- rapid response teams in every local authority area;
- free home care for the first four weeks after discharge from hospital;
- a shopping/home maintenance service in every area;
- more short breaks;
- joint resourcing and joint service management of services for older people.

In 2005 the Scottish Executive produced the *Joint Future Performance Information and Assessment Framework* (Scottish Executive, 2005a), which is intended to further promote the development of joint and integrated services. The overall purpose of the framework is to assist older people to live independent lives. The Scottish Executive Report Better Outcomes for Older People noted:

TMA4

> Older people are clear about the outcomes they want from services. They want:
>
> - to be helped to be more independent;
> - to have choice and control over how they manage their lives; and
> - to stay in their own homes whenever it is possible, with customised support.
>
> (Scottish Executive, 2005b)

And they do not particularly mind who provides the service. As their expectations of a better quality of life increase, they and their carers should be involved more effectively in designing and delivering joint services.

One of the key actions indicated in the *Joint Future Performance Information and Assessment Framework* is that local partnerships (comprising health, housing and social care partners) should have 'systematic arrangements for the collection of the views of people who use services' (Scottish Executive, 2005a). This key action links with another concern expressed in the framework – that there needs to be more focus on 'the specific needs of older people with additional needs because other than in the mental health field, few services are designed specifically for them'.

> **Box 6   The four national Joint Future outcome targets are:**
> - Supporting more people at home, as an alternative to residential and nursing care, through locally agreed joint service developments.
> - Assisting people to lead independent lives through reducing inappropriate hospital admissions, reducing time spent inappropriately in hospital, and enabling supported and faster discharges from hospital.
> - Ensuring people receive an improved quality of care through faster access to services and better quality services.
> - Better involvement and support of carers.
>
> (Clackmannanshire Joint Future Management Group Report, 2005)

 *Update Introduction Cont.*

1.2 What are community care services?

Community care can be seen as referring to social work services for adults. Community care services are not, however, confined to the provision of services in the community, they also include residential care. What community care services are depends on the needs of a given individual. There are three main groups of people who might be in need of community care services and some individuals will be in more than one group. These are:

- older people
- people with physical or learning disabilities
- people with mental health illness.

Activity 1 will help you to explore what community care services cover.

Allow about 30 minutes

Website

Activity 1   Community care services

Following the link from this activity on the course website read the Law Resource summary about the Social Work (Scotland) Act ~~1965~~ *1968* and make notes on the following questions:

1   How are community care services defined in the legislation?

2   What scope is there for geographical differences in service provision?

Comment

Community care services are defined in Part II of the Social Work (Scotland) Act 1968 as including residential care, domiciliary care and residential care with nursing. Social workers are involved in the assessment of need using a broad range of legislation. Some legislation, for example section 12A(1) of the Social Work (Scotland) Act 1968, places a statutory duty on local authorities to assess the needs of any person who may be in need of community care services. While the Act speaks of 'the local authority', it is usual for such assessments to be undertaken by the social work department.

One of the difficulties, however, about operating within a system that allows for discretion in the exercise of legislative options is the possibility that the interpretation placed on the local authority's responsibilities may be different in each area. Services are being provided from finite budgets, which will vary depending on the fiscal decisions (i.e. involving financial matters) of each set of councillors. Thus a service user may find that a service available to them in one local authority is not available when they move to another authority's area a few miles away.

A key recommendation of the Joint Future Group that was implemented by the Scottish Executive was free personal care. This was introduced in July 2002 by the Community Care and Health (Scotland) Act 2002. Personal care is free to those aged 65 and over and nursing care (in a care home) is free to anyone who needs it. There is still a charge for accommodation and food, subject to ability to pay.

Box 7   Free personal care

Section 1 of the Community Care and Health (Scotland) Act 2002 makes it clear that local authorities cannot charge for personal care.

'Personal care' means care which relates to the day-to-day physical tasks and needs of the person cared for (as for example, but without prejudice to that generality, to eating and washing) and to mental processes related to those tasks and needs (as for example, but without prejudice to that generality, to remembering to eat and wash).

(Section 2, Regulation of Care (Scotland) Act 2001)

---

see update.

However, free personal care has not been without its problems and recently the Health Committee of the Scottish Parliament carried out a review into the implementation of free personal care.

The Health Committee published its findings in 2006 (see Box 8).

Box 8   Findings of the Health Committee on free personal care

The Health Committee's review found that free personal care had:

1 provided greater security and dignity to many elderly people

2 allowed them to be cared for more readily at home

3 assisted their carers

4 reduced delayed discharges, thus freeing up NHS resources

5 largely ended disputes between local authorities and health boards over the care of elderly people

6 led to fewer complaints being reported to the Ombudsman about care of the elderly in Scotland than in England and Wales

7 prompted consideration to be given to the development of elderly care policy in England and Wales

8 in the main, been introduced swiftly and comprehensively

Problems that could undermine the effectiveness of free personal care included:

1 questions about the funding formula put in place by the Scottish Executive

2 the operation of 'waiting lists' for free personal care by half of all local authorities

3 a failure by the Scottish Executive to enforce clear guidance on key aspects of eligibility, such as the preparation of meals

4 the level of free personal care funding, which is not increasing in line with inflation

5 a lack of clarity regarding the date from which payments are required to be made, which could create a financial incentive for local authorities to delay assessments

6 continuing confusion over what is covered by the policy.

(Health Committee of the Scottish Parliament, 2006)

The Scottish Executive review also found that there were 4,000 people on waiting lists. Scotland's 32 local councils have told the executive that they are £70 million short of what is required to meet the full cost of free personal care. Members of the Scottish Parliament (MSPs) have condemned the waiting lists, introduced by 15 councils, as unacceptable and demanded that the loophole in the law which allowed waiting lists should be closed. The report also recommended that the Care Commission be funded centrally rather than from fees from local authorities and it said more use should be made of direct payments to people who organised their own care (BBC News, 2007).

Capability Scotland, Scotland's leading disability organisation, in order to inform its submission to the Health Committee Care for the Elderly Inquiry conducted some research on the extent to which users of their services of whom few were aged 65 or over were in receipt of free personal care. Their interest in the free personal care policy related to the possible extension of free personal care to those aged under 65. Capability Scotland reported that almost 20 per cent of participants with a disability, medical condition or long-term illness had to make some payment for their personal care with the majority paying between £10 and £30 per week; 6 per cent were paying more than £50 per week (Capability Scotland, 2006). They also found some evidence that there is inconsistency in what is charged, the levels of fees being charged and means testing. Capability Scotland also argued that the funding of care packages for disabled people was a funding maze made complex for service providers as well as individuals. The Health Committee is continuing to review the policy of free personal care.

It is important that social workers have a clear understanding of the differing duties placed on local authorities within the legislative framework of community care. Before exploring the legal framework of community care, however, it is useful to consider the place and significance of community care plans.

In 1998 the Scottish Office published *Modernising Community Care: An Action Plan*, which stated:

> People who use services and, more importantly, potential users must be better informed about community care if they are to have confidence in the services they receive and those who arrange and provide them. Local statutory organisations must develop better information for users about:
>
> - the types of services available and which agencies provide them;
>
> - how to qualify for these services;
>
> - the cost of services and any charges which may apply; and
>
> - the choices available, including how housing and support services can be combined to meet users' needs.
>
> (Scottish Office, 1998a, p. 41)

Local authorities are required to prepare and review community care plans. Plans have to be published at three-yearly intervals and reviewed annually. Under section 5A of the Social Work (Scotland) Act 1968 (as inserted by section 52 of the NHS and Community Care Act 1990) local authorities are also required to consult on their plans (or revisions to plans); the Community Care Plans (Consultation) Directions 1993 require that consultation includes organisations representing the independent sector and that the plans indicate the method of consultation. The local authority must also consult with health authorities, representative service user and carer organisations.

The plan should outline existing and planned services and should cover the needs of:

- older people
- people with disabilities
- people with learning disabilities
- people with mental health problems
- people with drug or alcohol problems
- people affected by HIV/AIDS
- people affected by progressive illnesses
- carers (including young carers).

The community care plan should also include:

- agreements and protocols with other agencies, including the requirements of the Joint Future Group
- the needs for each client group and how they are to be met
- identification of unmet needs
- details of services which the local authority may have a duty to provide
- details of from where the local authority intends to purchase services
- details of who has been consulted
- details of how the local authority intends to comply with the objectives of community care
- details of how the local authority is complying with the requirement for better and quicker decision making.

Community care plans are a statement of intent rather than a legally binding document and local authorities are free to deviate from their plans. Some information has to be included, particularly in relation to the Joint Future Group, but some information is optional. Copies of the plans should be available on the web and from libraries as well as the local authority's offices.

Website

Allow about 1 hour

Activity 2   Community care plans

Either use the direct.gov link in the Directory on the course website to access your local community care plan or ask for a copy from your local authority or library. Make notes on the following questions:

1   What do you consider to be the most important aspects of the community care plan you have read and why?

2   What aspects of the community care plan do you think would be of particular importance for service users and their carers?

Comment

While community care plans are local documents, as noted above, they must contain certain information and ought to be produced in consultation with the local community. The emphasis on the local can lead to variations in provision and service delivery across Scotland which is revealed by the annual reporting arrangements and monitoring. Part of the process whereby community care plans are produced should involve consultation with the local community, including with service users and carers groups. Some of the key aspects of the Clackmannanshire community care plan are reproduced in Box 9.

Box 9   Joint Future developments in Clackmannanshire

- Annual report to the Scottish Executive Joint Future Unit for evaluation.
- All Clackmannanshire community care funding is in a joint 'pot'.
- A single shared assessment process has been introduced and is based on Clackmannanshire Council's Community Care Information System (CCIS).
- Learning disability nurses are co-located in a social services base linking with the community learning disability team.
- Access to health and local authority services, including housing and adaptations for people with disabilities, are being addressed through joint work on the Forth Valley Area-wide strategies and the Local Housing and Homelessness strategies.
- Augmented home care and rapid response home care provisions have been extended to all service user care groups.
- A Joint Future Consultation exercise on effective consultation with service users and carers resulted in a good practice guide for implementation.
- Carers' assessments have been developed and community-based respite care provisions have increased.

You might find it useful to look at community care plans from different local authorities; it can be enlightening to examine the differences between them.

1.3 The legal framework of community care

The law relating to care in the community is mainly contained in the Social Work (Scotland) Act 1968, which has been substantially amended by subsequent legislation. Sections 5A and B, 6A, 12A–C, and 13A and B of this Act were all inserted as a result of the National Health Service and Community Care Act 1990. The Community Care (Direct Payments) Act 1996 added sections 12B and 12C, which have now been amended by the Community Care and Health (Scotland) Act 2002. This Act has also amended the law on carers' rights by adding new sections 12AA and 12AB into the Social Work (Scotland) Act 1968. The Social Work (Scotland) Act 1968 remains the primary legislation for community care service provision by local authorities. Table 1 clarifies this.

Table 1   Changes to Social Work (Scotland) Act 1968 by the National Health Service and Community Care Act 1990

Section in NHS and Community Care Act	New provision in Social Work (Scotland) Act	What it did
s51	s5	Gave the Secretary of State the power to issue 'directions' to local authorities on how they should exercise their functions
s52	s5A	Local authorities to publish community care plans
s52	s5B	Improved complaints procedure for social work departments
s53	s6	Added powers to Scottish Office to inspect care facilities
s54	s6A	Secretary of State may hold public inquiry into social work functions
s55	s12A	Assessment of needs (further amended by the Community Care and Health (Scotland) Act 2002)
s56	s13A	Social work department given power to pay for nursing home places
s56	s13B	Gave local authorities power to provide after-care, to help prevent illness and to care for ill people
s57	s6A	Stopped the DSS [Department of Social Security] from paying for people in registered homes after 1.4.93
s58	s92A	Established new Mental Illness Specific Grant for new projects of mental health, dementia and head injury — *No longer exists see update.*

(McKay and Patrick, 1995, p. 5)

In this block references will be made to the Social Work (Scotland) Act 1968 rather than the National Health Service Community Care Act 1990 and while much of the law relating to care in the community is to be found in the Social Work (Scotland) Act 1968, other statutory provisions are important. Box 10 provides a list of key statutes governing this area of practice.

Relevant legislation Relating to Community Care for Adults.

Box 10 Legislation relating to care in the community

- National Assistance Act 1948
- National Health Service (Scotland) Act 1978
- Social Work (Scotland) Act 1968 (as amended by the National Health Service and Community Care Act 1990, the Community Care (Direct Payments) Act 1996 and the Community Care and Health (Scotland) Act 2002)
- Chronically Sick and Disabled Persons Act 1970 (as amended by the Chronically Sick and Disabled Persons (Scotland) Act 1972)
- Mental Health (Care and Treatment) (Scotland) Act 2003
- Disabled Persons (Services, Consultation and Representation) Act 1986
- Adults with Incapacity (Scotland) Act 2000
- Regulation of Care (Scotland) Act 2001
- Community Care and Health (Scotland) Act 2002

There is also a range of Scottish Office and Scottish Executive Guidance that provides clarification of the policies and procedures related to the implementation of care in the community. This includes:

Print off Copies

1991	*Care Management and Assessment: Practitioners' Guide*
1991	*Care Management and Assessment: Managers' Guide*
1996	*Respite Care*
1996	*Care Programme Approach*
1998	*Community Care Needs of Frail Older People*
1998	*Modernising Community Care*
2001	*Guidance on Single Shared Assessment of Community Care Needs*
2003	*Direct payments: Policy and Practice Guidance*
2004	*Guidance on Care Management in Community Care*
2006	*Joint Performance Information and Assessment Framework*

 See update

A full and up-to-date list of community care circulars is available on the Scottish Executive Health Department website (www).

It is likely that service users and carers will fall within the scope of a number of statutory provisions. Activity 3 illustrates this.

Allow about 20 minutes   **Activity 3   Miss Campbell's story**

Read the following case study and list the matters that you think ought to concern the social worker involved in Miss Campbell's case and what you think her needs are, including those that you consider are already being met.

> Miss Campbell (81) lives alone in a two-room apartment on the third floor of a block of flats. She has angina and severe arthritis, which cause her to be confined to her home unless she has someone to accompany her. She currently receives the services of a home help for two hours twice a week, 'meals on wheels' three days a week and is visited every second Thursday by the district nurse, who baths her. Her niece, who is in regular employment, visits every evening and frequently stays overnight when Miss Campbell feels particularly distressed. Recently, Miss Campbell has become increasingly confused and on several occasions has allowed her sink to overflow, causing damage to her neighbour's ceiling.

Comment

It is clear that Miss Campbell has a range of needs that must be met if she is to continue living at home. Some of these are already being met: for example, by meals on wheels and the district nurse. However, as well as housing, the level of support might now be an issue. While considering these matters, the social worker would want to talk with Miss Campbell and her niece about what they would ideally like to happen.

Table 2 illustrates the range of legislation potentially applicable in this situation.

Table 2 Applicable legislation in Miss Campbell's case

Issue	Legislation	Responsible agency
Provision of home help	Section 14 of Social Work (Scotland) Act 1968	Local authority
Meals on wheels	Section 2 of the Chronically Sick and Disabled Persons Act 1970	Local authority
Bathing by district nurse	National Health Service (Scotland) Act 1978	Health board
Care provided by niece	Social Work (Scotland) Act 1968 as amended by Community Care and Health (Scotland) Act 2002	Local authority
Miss Campbell's confusion	Mental Health (Care and Treatment) (Scotland) Act 2003 and/or Adults with Incapacity (Scotland) Act 2000	Local authority or other appropriate individual
Inaccessibility of home	Chronically Sick and Disabled Persons Act 1970 – for aids and adaptations. Housing (Scotland) Act 1987 – for possible change of tenancy	Local authority
Free personal care	Community Care and Health (Scotland) Act 2002	Local authority

In order to best meet the needs of service users, it is important that social workers are able to work productively and creatively with other agencies. This legislation requires social work departments to undertake assessments on any person whom they consider to be in need of community care services. The Social Work (Scotland) Act 1968 covers the following groups:

- people with physical disabilities
- people with learning disabilities
- people with mental health problems
- people with HIV/AIDS
- people with addiction problems
- people with dementia
- older people with physical and other needs.

The needs of children under 16 are not specifically addressed by this legislation, but if they are carers, they now have the same rights as adults under sections 12AA and AB of the Social Work (Scotland) Act 1968. Their needs can also be addressed under sections 23 and 24 of the Children (Scotland) Act 1995 or by other legislation such as the Chronically Sick and Disabled Persons Act 1970. So community care services include services other than services for children, provided under Part II of the Social Work (Scotland) Act 1968 and sections 25, 26 and 27 of the Mental Health (Care and Treatment (Scotland) Act 2003. Next we look at the centrality of assessment and care management in this field.

Assessment

The process of assessment within the community care context is not contained in statute. While the mandate for practice is to be found in the Social Work (Scotland) Act 1968 the detail of how to carry out an assessment is to be found in guidance – similarly in relation to care management (see next section). Section 12A(1) of the Social Work (Scotland) Act 1968 states:

> Where it appears to a local authority that any person for whom they are under a duty or have a power to provide, or to secure the provision of, community care services may be in need of any such services, the authority –
>
> (a)   shall make an assessment of the needs of that person for those services; and
>
> (b)   shall then decide having regard to the results of that assessment and taking account
>
> > (i)   where it appears to them that a person ('the carer') provides a substantial amount of care on a regular basis for that person, of such care as is being so provided; and
> >
> > (ii)   in so far as it is reasonable and practicable to do so, both of the views of the person whose needs are being assessed and of the views of the carer (provided that in either case, there is a wish, or as the case may be, a capacity to express a view)
>
> whether the needs of that person call for the provision of any such services.

The requirements to take account of the amount of care being provided and the views of the carer and the service user were introduced by the Community Care and Health (Scotland) Act 2002. What, however, are the practice implications of the above provision? The guidance contained in Care Management and Assessment: Practitioners' Guide (Scottish Office Social Work Services Group, 1991) makes it clear that such assessments should be as comprehensive as possible, identifying the full range of needs and keeping a record of any that cannot be met and the reasons for the decisions.

See update.

One of the key recommendations in the Joint ~~Future Group~~ *Outcomes Team* report in 2000, which is now central to social work practice, is the single shared assessment (see Box 11). There is a single point of entry to community care services. This is to ensure that a single, structured approach to the assessment is promoted. The aim is for less bureaucracy, duplication and delay, with information being shared between professionals and agencies appropriately and with outcomes accepted by fellow professionals.

Box 11   The single shared assessment

The single shared assessment:

- is person-centred and needs-led
- relates to level of need
- is a process, not an event
- seeks information once
- has a lead professional who coordinates documents and shares appropriate information (not necessarily a social worker)
- coordinates all contributions
- produces a single summary assessment of need
- actively involves people who use services and their carers
- is a shared process that supports joint working
- provides results acceptable to all agencies.

The single shared assessment has been available for older people since April 2002 and has gradually been implemented for other service user groups from April 2003 onwards.

The Guidance on single shared assessment sets out that:

- the needs of the service user are paramount
- there must be a more holistic and efficient approach to assessment
- assessors must be drawn from other professions, such as health and housing
- there must be a more systematic approach to the allocation of resources.

(Scottish Executive, 2001a)

References in this block to a community care assessment mean a single shared assessment. Please also note that although the block makes reference to 'social work departments', in some areas, social work may now be part of a bigger service such as housing and social work. These materials refer to a social worker carrying out this assessment, but you should be aware that in some local authority areas, in keeping with the philosophy of the single shared assessment, the assessment may be carried out by another professional.

Activity 4 looks at assessment. The *Guidance on Single Shared Assessment* (Scottish Executive, 2001a) states that informed consent to the assessment and information sharing should be sought from the service user as part of the assessment process. Where it is not possible to obtain informed consent, every effort should be made to obtain the past views and wishes of the service user and the service user's interests should be safeguarded through the involvement of a legal representative, specialist worker, carer or advocate.

Allow about 1 hour   ## Activity 4   Assessing need

Read Miss Campbell's case again and, as far as you are able, identify her needs in relation to each of the headings in the list in Box 12.

Box 12 Assessing need

Biographical details including religion, ethnicity and any physical or mental impairment.

Self-perceived needs starting from the applicant's own perception of their needs.

Self-care, which encompasses basic activities such as eating, dressing, bathing and mobility and tasks such as dealing with money, cooking and using the telephone.

Physical health – a health professional's assessment might be necessary.

Mental health – it will be important to know when and how to involve the general practitioner (GP), community psychiatric nurse, approved social worker/mental health officer or psychiatric consultant.

Use of medicines –problems associated with medicine usage may affect considerably the quality of life of individuals or their carers.

Abilities, attitudes and lifestyle – this involves identifying the resources of individuals themselves and their care networks, before considering what additional resources may be required. The assessment has to focus on what is important to the individual to target any intervention in a way that will have the maximum beneficial effect on their quality of life.

Race and culture

Personal history

Needs of carers – the service user's perception of his or her needs is likely to be heavily influenced by the capacity and willingness of carers to continue to care. Throughout the assessment process, carers should be fully aware of their entitlement, within the constraints of confidentiality, to be involved and to be consulted. Where this is not the case, carers should be offered a separate assessment of their own needs.

Social network and support

Care services

Housing

Finance – it is important to ensure that service users are in receipt of their full social security entitlements. Advice on handling money should also be seen as a standard part of any assessment, including the involvement of the Court of Protection as appropriate.

Transport

Risk

(Adapted from Scottish Office Social Work Services Group, 1991, pp. 58–9)

Comment

It is important that any assessment of Miss Campbell's needs should be as comprehensive as possible. Some may be met by the provision of services, while others will be met through the development of existing personal relationships. The list of headings in Box 12 gives an indication of how wide-ranging and detailed an assessment can be – it should be holistic and conducted in partnership with Miss Campbell and her niece. It is also important that the assessment remains 'needs-led' rather than 'resources-led'. This is a significant aspect of the rhetoric of the NHS and Community Care Act 1990, which amended the Social Work (Scotland) Act 1968, and it is part of the challenge for you as a social worker to attempt to ensure that this focus is maintained. This is not always easy as there are pressures within all agencies to work within finite resources.

Assessments are carried out using the authority of a number of different pieces of legislation, each providing the service user with a potential range of services. It is important to remember that local authorities may struggle to meet all of their legal duties due to lack of resources and this may mean that there is unmet need. This is where a commitment to and consideration of service users' and carers' rights is particularly important. Front-line workers might find themselves in a very difficult situation – support from colleagues and line managers will be important.

There is special provision for disabled people in the Act. Section 12A(4) of the Social Work (Scotland) Act 1968 provides that:

> Where a local authority are making an assessment under this section and it appears to them that the person concerned is a disabled person, they shall –
>
> (a)   proceed to make such a decision as to the services he requires as is mentioned in section 4 of the Disabled Persons (Services,

Consultation and Representation) Act 1986 without his requesting them to do so under that section; and

(b)   inform him that they will be doing so and of his rights under that Act.

Section 4 of the Disabled Persons (Services, Consultation and Representation) Act 1986 confers the right to an assessment with regard to the services outlined in section 2 of the Chronically Sick and Disabled Persons Act 1970. This right extends to both the disabled person and their carer.

Box 13 Services under the Chronically Sick and Disabled Persons Act 1970

These services include:

- practical assistance in the home
- provision of radio, television and library facilities
- provision of recreational and educational facilities
- provision of transport facilities
- adaptations to the home
- provision of holidays
- meals
- telephone, including any special equipment to enable the disabled person to use it.

Thus there is a duty to carry out a second assessment for a disabled person and this assessment is service-led in that it looks at need for the specific services contained in the 1970 Act.

It is clear from the above that there are significant resource considerations involved in the assessment process. To what extent is the availability of resources relevant to the local authority's assessment of need? In R v. Gloucestershire County Council, ex parte Barry [1997] 4 All ER 421, the House of Lords decided that a local authority was able to take resources into account when assessing needs under section 2 of the Chronically Sick and Disabled Persons Act 1970. This decision has given rise to considerable controversy. According to some commentators:

> Cash strapped local authorities, faced with growing demand, use eligibility criteria to tailor that demand to their resources. Eligibility criteria have been tightened as resources decrease further to restrict access to services. The House of Lords has now decided that this is lawful. Whether a disabled person has 'needs' as opposed to 'wants' will now depend, in part, on how much money a local authority has allocated to its community care budget.
>
> (Ashton and Gould, 1997, p. 23)

In this case the local authority was already providing services to Mr Barry, who had had a stroke and suffered from poor eyesight. Mr Barry was in receipt of a number of services, including meals on wheels and twice-weekly home care to help with shopping and cleaning. However, when faced with a serious financial shortfall, the local authority reduced its services. It was decided that the local authority could reduce or withdraw services to people in need but only after it had reassessed the need. And in reassessing need it could take into account its own changed circumstances – including resource constraints. So, even though the circumstances of the person in need were unchanged, the change in the local authority's financial situation would permit the withdrawal or curtailment of services, provided there had been a reassessment.

If the local authority is allowed to take resources into account, it can cap its liability to provide community care services, irrespective of the actual needs of 'persons in need' who live in the area. An assessment is designed to determine whether there is a need for community care services. Once this has been determined, the local authority is under a duty to decide which needs require the provision of services and what services will satisfy these needs. In addressing this last question, the local authority can take 'eligibility criteria' into account, which structure the local authority's discretion.

Despite the financial constraints facing local authorities, social workers should endeavour to engage with the assessment process within an overall context of empowerment and user involvement. Assessment should not be viewed as a bureaucratic event but as an inclusive and enabling process. The Practitioners' Guide states:

> At the end of the assessment, users should know:
> - who has taken the decision on eligibility;
> - which needs are, or are not, eligible for assistance and why;
> - which needs might be eligible for assistance from other care agencies;
> - when, and under what circumstances, they may request reassessment; and
> - the means of complaining if dissatisfied.
>
> (Scottish Office Social Work Services Group (1991), quoted by Coulshed and Orme, 1998, pp. 33–4)

See update!

55
61
63

Good for TMA

Listening to service users is important to shape their needs

The *Report of the 21st Century Social Work Review* argues for the delivery of personalised services with the service user at the 'centre as a participant in shaping the services they get' (Scottish Executive, 2006b). Later the report states 'successful services will only be possible if those who use them start to play a much larger role in assessing their own needs and devising their own plans, often through consultation with professionals' (Scottish Executive, 2006b). A complementary observation from a users and carers panel is cited in the report: 'We want to have trusting relationships with workers whom we can be confident have our interests at heart and can help us find our way through the "system"' (Scottish Executive, 2006b, p. 36).

Activity 5 asks you to look more closely at the various aspects of community care law.

Allow about 1 hour

Reader

Activity 5   Care in the community

Read Chapter 11, 'Care in the community', in the Reader and make notes on the following questions:

1   Is the section 12A assessment for community care services needs-led or service-led?

2   Is the duty to carry out a second assessment for disabled people usually fulfilled?

3   What additional rights do carers have under the Community Care and Health (Scotland) Act 2002?

4   Why have local authorities been ambivalent towards the development of direct payments?

Comment

The section 12A assessment for community care services is needs-led, having moved away from the previous model of slotting people into available services. However, the disabled person's assessment is service-led in that it looks for need for the specific list of services in the Chronically Sick and Disabled Persons Act 1970.

The duty to carry out this second assessment for disabled service users is not routinely fulfilled and of course most service users are unaware that they have a right to this assessment.

Carers, including those aged under 16 years, now have the right to an assessment at any time, not simply when the person they care for is having a community care assessment. The local authority also has a duty to advise carers of their right to request a carer's assessment.

Petch believes that local authorities have been ambivalent about the development of direct payments because they see them as a potential threat to the services provided by the local authority, such as day care services.

Once a person has been assessed as needing community care services, the next step might be the drawing up of a care plan – this leads to the issue of care management which the next section considers.

Care management

Since care management was introduced over a decade ago, community care policy has undergone significant change with much greater emphasis on empowering service users and carers, the promotion of joint working and the development of Joint Future. As noted before Joint Future aims to improve outcomes by enabling better and quicker access to services through a single shared assessment and more integrated approaches to the managing, financing and running of services.

The single shared assessment is central to good care management and both share the same commitment to being person-centred (Scottish Executive, 2001a, 4.3).

Box 14 What is care management?

Care management is:

- a process that includes assessing individual needs and tailoring services to meet those needs;

- focused on people with complex, or frequently or rapidly changing needs; and

- undertaken by a range of professionally qualified staff in social work and health, with appropriate training, skills and experience.

(Scottish Executive Joint Future Unit, 2004)

Good care management includes not just implementing a care plan but its monitoring and review (see Figure 1). People who use services and their carers should be actively involved and enabled to participate and care management should be available to all community care groups. Care managers need to recognise the rights of carers (under the Community Care and Health (Scotland) Act 2002) and the empowering potential of direct payments.

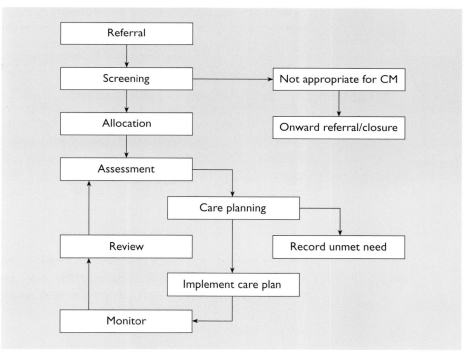

Figure 1   The process of care management (Aberdeen City Council, 2002)

The Guidance points out that the care programme approach (CPA) widely used in mental health services is a form of care management for people with severe and enduring mental illness who also have complex health and social care needs. People with mild to moderate mental health problems may not be eligible for CPA but they should be considered for care management where their community care needs are complex or frequently or rapidly changing (Scottish Executive Joint Future Unit, 2004).

People who should be considered for care management include those who:

- may require or are at risk of permanent admission to care homes or other long-stay care settings
- are being discharged from hospital or other care settings after a period of long-term care
- are being discharged following major intervention or serious illness requiring acute hospital care
- are experiencing severe mental or physical incapacity and loss of independence
- are terminally ill and may require palliative care
- are at high physical risk
- are in need of care and protection
- have complex needs or challenging behaviour where high level support is necessary or whose care arrangements are at risk of breaking down
- have rapidly or frequently changing need
- are highly dependent on the input of a carer
- are carers of people with complex needs whose own care needs mean they are unable to maintain their caring role and require services in their own right.

All appropriate to Case Study for TMA 4

Both assessment and care management raise the issue of working in partnership with service users and carers in order to ensure that any services provided are relevant and appropriately delivered.

1.4 Service users and carers

Service users and their experience of services and service delivery is at the very centre of social work policy and practice developments in Scotland. Progress has been made since the mid 1990s but there is still much to be done. Professionals might have their own views about how best to extend service user and carer involvement in service delivery. It is important to recognise that service users and carers also have a perspective on this issue.

Service users

Service users may prefer to make their own arrangements regarding the services they require; this might allow service users and their carers to exercise more control over the nature and timing of the service they need. The local authority, having agreed an assessment of need with a service user, may consider it more effective to make a payment directly to that service user in order that he or she may arrange to have his or her needs met. This provides some service users with an opportunity to have a package of care that is more responsive to their needs and to continue to exercise some control over their own lives. In order to facilitate the use of direct payments and enhance the degree of control service users can have over the quality and detail of the service they receive, section 12B of the Social Work (Scotland) Act 1968 was inserted by the Community Care (Direct Payments) Act 1996.

> ### Box 15 Direct payments
>
> Direct payments can only be made to those who are able and willing to manage such payments.
>
> Direct payments can only be made to people who have been assessed as needing community care services. (The Community Care and Health (Scotland) Act 2002 imposed a duty on local authorities to offer direct payments to anyone entitled to community care services from April 2004.) Research published by the Scottish Executive found that implementation of direct payments has been slow across Scotland (Ridley and Jones, 2002). Between 1996 and 2001 the research found only two mental health service users who were in receipt of direct payments, and generally knowledge about eligibility among service users and professionals was poor.
>
> Direct payments cannot be used to pay for services other than those for which the service user has been assessed.
>
> Direct payments cannot be made to people detained under the Mental Health (Care and Treatment) (Scotland) Act 2003 or who are subject to guardianship under the Adults with Incapacity (Scotland) Act 2000.
>
> A legally-appointed representative such as a guardian or an attorney is able to consent to direct payments on behalf of the person they are appointed to.
>
> Until December 2001, direct payments were available only to those aged 18 and over. This was reduced to age 16 and over. From the same date, parents of disabled children became entitled to receive direct payments in order to purchase services for their children.
>
> Direct payments may be used to buy services from the local authority.

Allow about 20 minutes

See update.

Website

Activity 6   Securing direct payments

Following the link from this activity on the course website, make notes on the process for securing direct payments for community care services.

Comment

The system of direct payments is gradually being expanded. Since June 2003 local authorities have been under a duty to offer direct payments to those who qualify and from April 2004 any person who qualified for community care services became eligible for direct payments, whether or not they are disabled.

In some circumstances, service users may find it more suitable to make their own arrangements regarding the services they require. A young physically disabled person may, for example, find the home care services available to her to be too inflexible to allow her to continue at work. She requires someone to be available each morning at 7.15 am to help with washing and dressing, but the home care worker from the local authority cannot guarantee to be there as she sometimes has to respond to emergencies. By being given the equivalent funding, the disabled person can employ someone who is contracted to meet her needs rather than those of an agency and thus take more control over her own life and exercise choice in service provision.

The Health Committee of the Scottish Parliament reviewed the use of direct payments in 2006 and its findings are in the same report as the findings relating to free personal care (Health Committee of the Scottish Parliament, 2006). The committee found that:

- The numbers in receipt of payments increased from 207 in 2001 to 1,438 in 2005 and the value of payments increased from £2.1 to £13.7 million. On this basis the 2002 Act can be judged to have been a success.
- Payments in Scotland are still running at half the level of England and Wales. There is also a wide variation in take-up across Scottish local authority areas.

The Health Committee is working to find ways to ensure that all local authorities fulfil their duties to service users in making available direct payments. The introduction of direct payments can be seen as a response to demands from service users and their carers to have more control over the services they receive. This is in keeping with the increasing emphasis on working in partnership with service users and their participation and inclusion.

Carers

Now called.
Self directed support
see update.

Family members who care are important to community care

In the research reviewed for the report *Whose Rights Are They Anyway? Carers and the Human Rights Act* four themes emerged (Carers UK, 2006). These are:

- Carers' rights are not adequately considered.
- Carers' rights are not real.
- Resources are inadequate to allow rights to be protected.
- Good practice need not be expensive.

There is, therefore, concern about what, in practice, has been the impact of recent legislation that has sought to focus professional practice on the needs, concerns and rights of carers as well as service users. Box 16 outlines legislation that is specifically concerned to address the needs of carers.

Box 16 Legislation relating to carers

The Disabled Persons (Services, Consultation and Representation) Act 1986 – required the local authority to have regard to the carer's ability to provide care when assessing the needs of a disabled service user.

The Community Care and Health (Scotland) Act 2002 – gave carers the right to an independent assessment emphasising that carers should seen as partners in providing care. It also gave carers under 16 the same right to an assessment as adults.

The Mental Health (Care and Treatment) (Scotland) Act 2003 – one of the ten principles underpinning the legislation is that carers should be recognised, with carers able to request an assessment of the service user's needs.

In addition the 'consultation with relevant others' principle of the Adults with Incapacity (Scotland) Act 2000 states that 'in determining if an intervention is to be made and, if so, what intervention is to be made, account should be taken of – (b) the views of the nearest relative and the primary carer of the adult in so far as it is reasonably practicable to do so' (para. 4). While the law appears to give carers new rights there are clearly problems regarding the realisation of these rights. This is considered in more detail later in the block when we focus on the situation facing particular groups of service users. Activity 7 provides you with the opportunity to explore the experiences of carers.

Allow about 40 minutes   ## Activity 7   Carers' rights

Website

Following the link from this activity to the course website, read the Carers UK report, *Whose Rights Are They Anyway? Carers and the Human Rights Act* and make notes on the following questions:

1   According to Carers UK how many carers are there in Scotland and what percentage are women?

2   What is the contribution of their caring activity?

3   What is the potential impact of the Human Rights Act 1998 on carers?

Comment

The report states that there are 481,579 carers in Scotland of whom 63 per cent are women. While the impact of becoming a carer can be life-changing it is also the case that carers are critical, for example in allowing older or disabled people to live independently and providing emotional support in the context of loss and bereavement. However, carers can themselves be vulnerable as a result of being committed to their caring responsibilities or the circumstances in which they continue to care. The impact of the Human Rights Act 1998 on carers has been disappointing. In theory while carers have more rights than ever before, their realisation is undermined by the realities of professional social work practice ('many carers do not receive any individual time with a social worker where they might be able to speak freely about what help they need', p. 14), carers' lack of knowledge of their rights, and inadequate resources. The report also argues that good practice need not be expensive and provides some examples ('St Helens in Merseyside runs a 24-hour carers' helpline which enables carers to be quickly identified in the case of an emergency', p. 16).

The Carers UK report makes a number of significant observations about professional practice across health and social care and later in this block we will return to some of these issues, for example the neglect of carers' rights. Activity 8, however, allows you to explore in more detail the issues facing carers and the kinds of support they need.

Activity 8   Caring

Allow about 1 hour

Audio CD

Listen to the interview with Isobel Allan, who is caring for her 26-year-old disabled daughter, and make notes on the following questions:

1   What difficulties has Isobel Allan experienced in caring for her daughter?

2   Why does she describe the independent living fund as 'brilliant'?

3   What does she see as the weaknesses of the care system?

4   What is required for the receipt of care services to be a positive and supportive experience?

5   Is there a good side to caring?

Comment

Isobel Allan describes different kinds of difficulties: knowing that you need respite care yet being reluctant to allow a stranger to come into your own home to care for your child; the absence of support once her daughter was no longer in 'special needs' education; and the effort required to find the right kind of services for her daughter. She found social work professionals unwilling to surrender their power and describes how her social worker was very directive and unwilling to consult and work with the family. Later she talks about how everything has to be planned – she cannot afford spontaneity. She describes the independent living fund as brilliant precisely because it provides 'control, choice and flexibility'. In contrast, the weaknesses of the care system lie in its prescriptive and bureaucratic approach so that carers need to be patient, know the system and be determined if they are going to get a good or appropriate service. She is also clear about what makes for a good service. This includes: continuity of carers (she talks about having a core group of carers so that if one is ill or on holiday someone else she and her daughter knows will come); the importance of understanding that you are coming into someone else's home and the need to respect the family and its privacy; and a mixture of warmth and respect for boundaries on the part of carers coming into your home. Isobel Allan finds it hard to comment on whether there is a good side to caring in that she says no one would choose to be a carer rather than, for example, a mother. However, she has to care for her daughter and her struggle to form an equal relationship with her – to do things with her and not just to her or for her – has been both very hard and very rewarding. She is anxious about the future especially as she does not think the system is in place to provide for her daughter as she has for the past twenty-six years.

It is interesting to note how important a sense of genuine partnership was for Isobel Allan; the relationship with the social worker did not get off to a good start but they worked through it. Similarly, partnership with carers who came into her home was important – hence the instructions and the clarity regarding boundaries. The 21st Century Social Work Review refers to how carers should be 'recognised as active partners and care providers, able to influence how services are designed, planned and delivered' (Scottish Executive, 2006b, p. 16).

Carers are often relatives and may have additional rights by virtue of that relationship. For example as parents they will have parental rights and responsibilities in relation to a child they are caring for. Some disabled people are in need of substantial care and support, for example someone born with a severe physical or learning disability; often it is the child's parents who provide such care. Many parents, however, assume that they may legally continue to make decisions after their child reaches the age of 16. However, parental responsibilities and rights end when the child reaches the age of 16. This means that parents lose the right to make legal decisions for their child, unless they take formal legal steps to acquire that right. A social worker might find themselves having to explain this, for example, to parents who have been caring for their disabled child since early childhood and who may react angrily to something that appears to them to be insensitive and inappropriate.

Before concluding, it is important to provide an overview of the legal framework of accountability before, in Sections 2, 3 and 4, exploring the situations that can arise when working with particular groups of people in need of community care services.

Accountability

In terms of community care a service user can complain about the way their assessment was carried out, or the decision about what services to provide, or the decision about how much they have to pay towards the cost of their services.

Among its requirements the Scottish Social Services Council (SSSC) expects social workers to:

- uphold public trust and confidence in social services
- be accountable for the quality of their work and take responsibility for maintaining and improving their knowledge and skills.

Many service users do not feel comfortable about complaining. This may be because they fear that there will be repercussions for them or simply because they are grateful for any provision and do not feel that it is appropriate to complain. This area of social work creates conflicts of interest for social workers, who may be aware when they carry out an assessment that the service user will not be offered services due to lack of resources. They will also be aware that most service users have no idea what their rights are unless they are given that information. If service users are to be empowered to feel comfortable about challenging decisions that affect them, social workers must give information about legal rights and must encourage service users to complain.

Under section 5B of the Social Work (Scotland) Act 1968 carers can complain about a local authority's failure to provide an assessment under sections 12AA and AB of the Social Work (Scotland) Act 1968 or about the conduct of the assessment. They can also complain on behalf of service users about services provided by local authorities including those provided in response to a carers' assessment. Under the National Health Service (Scotland) Act 1978 both service users and carers have a right to complain about any services provided by NHS Scotland.

Box 17 Making a complaint

Make a complaint through the local authority complaints procedure. This complaints procedure covers all social work services for adults and children. Some service users do not perceive this internal complaints procedure to be independent or impartial.

Make a complaint to the Scottish Public Services Ombudsman, but this applies only if there has been maladministration.

Seek judicial review through the Court of Session, but this can be costly and take a long time.

Many service users may be afraid to complain or take action in case their services are removed, even though legally this cannot happen. Individual workers and the local authority have a responsibility to ensure that service users are advised about this.

Recent guidance on single shared assessment makes it clear that charges for services should be made clear in any material produced and should be clearly explained to users as part of their assessment. The care plan should include a written explanation of any charges, and users should be advised of their rights to make representations.

1.5 Conclusion

The law on care in the community is to be found in a range of statutes and it is this fragmentation that makes it difficult to fully understand. This complexity is compounded by the fact that it is clear the local authority has some discretion in relation to the range of services it provides, as well as the level of those services. However, some people, for example disabled people, have a right to an assessment and this assessment must take into account the ability of a relevant carer to continue caring for the disabled person. The process of conducting an assessment should be open and clearly explained to the service user. Although the legislation now requires the views of the service user to be taken into account, there may still be an issue about how much the service user is empowered to participate in the assessment process.

In the next section you will explore this legislative framework more fully in relation to the needs and interests of older people.

Key points

- The provision of community care services is regulated by a number of statutes, although the Social Work (Scotland) Act 1968 is the main piece of legislation.
- Assessment of need is central to the system of care in the community.
- Single shared assessment entails professionals working together across professional boundaries in order to secure quality social care services
- The local authority is not allowed to take resources into account when assessing need.
- Care management is an integral part of professional practice in community care
- Social workers should work in partnership with service users and carers, empowering them and promoting their rights.

2 Older people

For this section you need:

- audio CD
- course website access for online activities
- Reader, Chapter 13.

Core questions

- What is the role of the social worker in the provision of care in the community for older people?
- What is the legal framework for the protection of older people from exploitation and abuse?
- What care options exist to enable older people to live as independently as possible?

2.1 Introduction

Age appears in a number of statutes as a basis on which intervention may be required. For example, section 94(1) of the Social Work (Scotland) Act 1968 defines a person in need as being 'in need of care and attention arising out of infirmity, youth or age'. However, there is little specific legislation that applies to older people. There is not an 'Older People (Scotland) Act' on the statute book offering a similar range of provisions to the Children (Scotland) Act 1995. However, there are proposals currently before the Scottish Parliament for a Commissioner for Older People in order to safeguard and promote their rights and interests. That said, it is not the person's age that is the defining feature, but their potential vulnerability. So the range of legislation applicable to older people is related to specific issues such as mental health, disability, and so on.

See update - No Commissioner.

For social workers, it is not just a question of being aware of their statutory powers and duties in relation to older people. It is also a question of acknowledging the 'personhood' of older people they are working with, and treating them with respect as well as care (Kitwood, 1997). As part of the 21st Century Social Work Review, the Scottish Executive asked the Social Work Research Centre at the University of Stirling to review the evidence base for effective social work with older people. The main findings of this research are summarised in Box 18.

> **Box 18 Effective social work with older people**
>
> Age in itself is not a problem, pathology or indication of need ... Older people do not require social work support simply because of their age.
>
> Social work with older people cannot be considered effective unless older people themselves are satisfied with it. Service users want to be listened to and respected as individuals. Many

older people share traditional social work values, such as a concern for relationships, and appreciate social work skills. The social work *process* is important, as well as the outcome.

Social care with older people is more effective when its intended outcomes are identified at an early stage – during assessment – and built into care planning. Older people must be closely involved in the process, with outcomes based on their wishes and priorities as far as possible.

Older people like services which support them in various aspects of their lives, not just personal care and relationship needs. Low-level preventive services are valued.

Effective social work with older people should focus on intensive care management with those who have complex, fluctuating and/ or rapidly changing needs. Pressure to manage budgets and establish eligibility must not reduce social workers' capacity to engage with the older person and use the full repertoire of their skills in a holistic way.

Social workers bring a unique mix of skills and expertise to situations of complexity, uncertainty and conflict. These include a 'whole system' view, engaging with the older person's biography, supporting individuals and families through crises associated with loss or transition, helping to ameliorate the practical impact of change and challenging poor practice.

Social workers must work creatively with risk. They need finely-tuned skills to achieve the 'right' balance between promoting self determination and independence for the older person while, at the same time, ensuring that vulnerable individuals have adequate protection.

There is much scope for a positive, proactive approach to social work with older people, for example through income maximisation, promoting individual strengths and capacity, and helping people rebuild confidence and networks following loss or change. Anti-ageism is an essential element, while issues of gender, race, class and ethnicity must be taken into account.

(Kerr et al., 2005)

Social workers may have to use the legislative framework to assist older people who are at risk of harm – either to themselves or others – or to promote their welfare. We have already looked at some of the relevant legislation in the previous section but Box 19 summarises three statutes that are important in this task.

See update...

Now Adult Support and protection Act 2007

Box 19 The law and older people

National Assistance Act 1948

This legislation is potentially useful as a means of providing services on an emergency basis. Section 47 provides for compulsory admission to a residential home or hospital where any persons who are 'suffering from grave chronic disease or, being aged or infirm or physically incapacitated, are living in insanitary conditions, and they are unable to devote to themselves, and are not receiving from other persons, proper care and attention'.

The legislation sets out a procedure whereby an older person who is considered to be a risk to themselves or others may be compulsorily removed to a more suitable environment. Clearly, this involves health and social work professionals in value-based judgements about the quality of life of an older person who, by virtue of his or her circumstances, may be unable to play an active role in decision making. This legislation tends to be used infrequently and has been the subject of review by the Scottish Law Commission.

Social Work (Scotland) Act 1968

Under section 12 of this Act, local authority social work departments have a duty to 'promote social welfare by making available advice, guidance and assistance on such a scale as may be appropriate for their area'. As you will have noted earlier, section 12A places a duty on local authorities to provide assessments of need for anyone they consider may be in need of 'community care services'.

The Adults With Incapacity (Scotland) Act 2000

The Adults With Incapacity (Scotland) Act 2000 specifies five principles which must be followed in applying the Act: intervention must be for the benefit of the adult; it must be the least restrictive option; account must be taken of the 'present and past wishes and feelings of the adult'; account must be taken of the views of relevant others including the nearest relative and primary carer; and the adult must be encouraged to 'exercise whatever skills he has concerning his property, financial affairs or personal welfare' (section 1 of the Adults With Incapacity (Scotland) Act 2000).

Key Act along with ASPA (2007) + SWSA (68) s12

The Act provides a number of mechanisms for protecting the interests of adults with incapacity. It allow adults while still capable to grant someone a 'power of attorney' over their affairs, that is to take decisions on their behalf if they should become incapable. It also allows for the sheriff court to make intervention and guardianship orders in order to allow decisions to be made in relation to an adult with incapacity.

An older person who for example has dementia or a learning disability may not be able to make decisions about their future care and is, as a consequence, vulnerable to harming themselves and possibly other people. If the adult, while they still had

See for TMA 4

capacity, has not already made an appropriate power of attorney the sheriff court could make a guardianship order, usually with the local authority as guardian, which would allow decisions to be made about the person's place of residence and any medical treatment they may require. Any treatment would still require the person's consent, unless the guardianship order gave authority to the guardian to give such consent. This would allow the guardian to arrange to have the older person admitted to a residential or nursing home where their care needs could best be met. It would also allow the guardian to make such welfare decisions on behalf of the person as the order permitted.

The rest of this section explores three areas:

- the provision of appropriate care in the community for older people
- the protection of older people from exploitation, abuse or harm
- the provision of alternative care for older people.

2.2 Provision of appropriate care in the community

With the right services people can remain at home

While there are large numbers of older people who live fulfilled and independent lives within their communities, there is a significant group who, as a consequence of increasing frailty, decreasing mobility or deteriorating physical or mental health, find it increasingly difficult to cope. As with any other group of service users, social workers seek to build on the strengths people have and to provide such services as may be appropriate to allow the continuation of an independent existence. In order to assist an older person to remain in their own home, there is a range of legislative provisions. Activity 9 illustrates this.

Allow about 45 minutes

Activity 9   Community care assessment

Website

Following the link from this activity on the course website, read the relevant Law Resource summaries and then the following case study. Make notes on the questions that follow using that information.

Mohammed Khan (86) lives with his son Iqbal (57), his daughter-in-law Sumaiya (51) and their three teenage children in a large detached house that is owned by Iqbal and his wife. Mr Khan came to Scotland at the age of 37 and built up a successful business empire that is now run by his three sons. His wife died five years ago and he misses her very much. Until last year Mr Khan was physically active and mentally alert. He enjoyed socialising with other Muslim men in his community and was an important elder in the local mosque. Earlier this year he fell outside his house and broke his hip. He spent several weeks in hospital, which he found very difficult, and his recovery from his accident has been slow.

Mr Khan has great difficulty in walking and now finds it hard to get around the family home with its many stairs and long walks between rooms. He tires after walking more than a few steps, has some difficulty dressing himself and is becoming increasingly forgetful. He is also lonely, as he is rarely able to go out. He now only visits the mosque when the other family members attend.

His daughter-in-law Sumaiya is a successful lawyer who runs her own practice, while Iqbal is involved in the family business in partnership with his brothers. The couple have a strong sense of duty to their father but are finding it increasingly difficult to provide care for him. They approach the social work department for a community care assessment.

---

1   How might the law be used to provide a comprehensive assessment of Mr Khan's needs?

2   In particular, what legislation would you make use of to offer effective support to Mr Khan?

Comment

The assessment would be undertaken using section 12A of the Social Work (Scotland) Act 1968. This allows the social worker to assess the full range of needs Mr Khan may have. Consideration should be given as to whether an interpreter might be necessary for Mr Khan. Even if he is comfortable in using English, second language skills can be lost when people are confused and forgetful. Mr Khan's mobility problems may be helped by the provision of a walking aid and handrails to the internal stairways in his home. If his bedroom is on a different floor from the living area, an electric stair lift may help. All of these services can be provided under the provisions of section 2 of the Chronically Sick and Disabled Persons Act 1970. Given the family's financial circumstances, it is likely that at least some of the costs will be met by them.

The same legislation could be used to provide transport to take Mr Khan to visit his friends at the mosque or to provide him with a short holiday. Both these options would help address his increasing social isolation. The problems he has with dressing, and with basic housekeeping skills such as cooking, could be met by providing him with home care services under section 14 of the Social Work (Scotland) Act 1968. Clearly, it would be most important that any services were provided in a sensitive way taking account of the cultural, social and religious background of Mr Khan and his family.

It may be that the local authority, having assessed Mr Khan's need for community care services, finds it impossible to meet some needs in a way that is acceptable to the service user and his family. The times when a home care worker is available may not fit with the family's routine and the local authority may have difficulty in identifying a suitable worker. It may be a better practical arrangement for the family to hire their own care worker through one of the increasing number of private providers. Such a private contractual arrangement may prove to be no more expensive than their assessed contribution to the provision of the service by the local authority.

As part of the overall assessment, the local authority would also take account of the needs of Mr Khan's carers, that is, his son and daughter-in-law. Under the Social Work (Scotland) Act 1968, the carers are entitled to ask for an assessment, and if assessed, to have their ability to continue to care assessed and their needs as carers taken into account. With effect from September 2002, the Community Care and Health (Scotland) Act 2002 imposed a duty on local authorities to advise carers of their right to an assessment. It should not automatically be assumed that carers will wish to, or are able to, continue in this role indefinitely. Despite the fact that this family is financially secure, the social worker should also ensure that Mr Khan is in receipt of any welfare benefits to which he is entitled.

Carers are often under a great deal of stress. Good practice requires that proper regard be taken of carers' need for support, including respite care. Such supportive practice might result in a better quality of life for all concerned, as well as avoiding the significant financial and psychological costs associated with going into residential care. It should also be remembered that some carers are young and assume substantial caring responsibilities for older relatives and younger siblings (Tatum and Tucker, 1998).

A significant number of people may at some point in their lives be confused and unable to make decisions. The condition may not be too serious (for example, the result of illness) and all that may be required is help and support in overcoming the difficulties. However, the condition may arise from a profound learning disability, mental illness or dementia and may render the person quite incapable of understanding what is happening and consequently unable to make decisions and give instructions about what should be done on their behalf. Such people are deemed in the terms of the Adults with Incapacity (Scotland) Act 2000 to be 'incapable' and the law provides a number of ways of addressing the problems presented. Activity 10 helps you to consider these different legal provisions and the circumstances in which they might be used.

Allow about 50 minutes

Website

Activity 10   Incapacity

Following the link from this activity on the course website, read the Law Resource and make notes on the following questions:

1   What does the law mean by 'incapable'?

2   What principles apply to any intervention under the Act?

3   What provisions are made by the law to address the problems presented by people who are unable to manage their own affairs or make decisions about their lives?

Comment

The law defines 'incapable' as 'incapable of acting or making decisions or communicating decisions or understanding decisions or retaining the memory of decisions in relation to any particular matter, by reason of mental disorder or of inability to communicate due to physical disability'.

Obviously, there is a range within this definition, from people whose inability only relates to decisions about very complex matters, to those who are not able to communicate any decisions. The law needs to be able to respond to these differences and to do so in a way that maximises opportunities for people to have a say in their own lives. The Adults with Incapacity (Scotland) Act 2000 makes it clear that capacity is 'task specific' and that any intervention must be the least restrictive option. Box 20 lists the five overarching principles.

Remember + learn these.

Need for exam

> **Box 20   Adults with Incapacity (Scotland) Act 2000 – the five principles**
>
> - Intervention must be for the benefit of the adult.
> - The intervention must be the least restrictive option.
> - The past and present view of the adult must be sought.
> - The views of other relevant persons must be sought.
> - The adult must be encouraged to use and develop those decision-making skills that he or she has.

The Act provides a number of mechanisms for addressing problems presented by people who are unable to manage their own affairs. It allows adults to anticipate the possibility of their being incapable by allowing them to appoint continuing attorneys and welfare attorneys who will then be able to take decisions on their behalf. Any person who is considered incapable of making significant decisions about their life can be protected using a range of civil law options, including intervention orders and guardianship orders.

Any person can also bring to the attention of the Public Guardian any concerns about the financial welfare of an incapable adult and the Public Guardian has a duty to investigate. Similarly concerns about their personal welfare can be brought to the attention of the local authority in the first instance and then the Mental Welfare Commission – both have a duty to investigate.

There are limitations to all these appointments in that the Act requires that any intervention must benefit the adult and must be the least restrictive option. Powers will be tailored to the needs of each individual. This is explored in Activity 11.

Allow about 45 minutes   ## Activity 11   Decision making

Using the information you acquired in completing Activities 9 and 10, examine Table 3 and then consider which type of appointment might be the most suitable in the case examples listed after the table.

Table 3   Who can act?

Appointments	Who are they?	Who appoints them?	What powers do they have?
Department for Work and Pensions (DWP) appointee	Any appropriate person – often a relative or carer	DWP	Power to claim, collect and spend welfare benefits
Managers of establishments (from April 2003)	–	–	Power to administer patients' fund when the patients are residents of psychiatric and learning disability hospitals, nursing and residential homes
Power of attorney (made prior to April 2001)	Anyone chosen by the person (often relative or solicitor)	The person before they become incapacitated	Power to deal with financial affairs subject to any specifications in the deed appointing them
Continuing power of attorney (made from April 2001 onwards)	Anyone chosen by the person (often a relative or solicitor)	The person before they become incapacitated	Power to deal with financial affairs as specified in the deed. May come into effect immediately upon registration with the Public Guardian or upon certification of incapacity and registration with the Public Guardian
Welfare power of attorney (made from April 2001 onwards)	Anyone chosen by the person	The person before they become incapacitated	Power to deal with welfare decisions as specified in the deed. May include medical consent. Only comes into effect after loss of capacity and registration with the Public Guardian
Authority to intromit with funds	Any appropriate individual	Authority from the Public Guardian	Power to open a designated bank account and pay bills as specified in the authority
Intervention orders	Anyone claiming an interest in the finance or welfare of an adult with incapacity	Person authorised by the order	Made by sheriff court and authorises one-off decisions

| Guardianship orders | Welfare and/or financial powers. Could be the social work department for welfare powers and solicitor for financial powers | Sheriff court | Specific powers granted by the court in accordance with the overarching principles in the 2000 Act. Those who were appointed tutors-*dative* or curators *bonis* prior to April 2002 became guardians from April 2002 with the powers that they already had. From April 2002 mental health guardians already appointed under the MH(S)A 1984 became guardians with the restricted powers they already had, i.e. power to require person to: live in a specified place; attend for medical treatment and various other purposes; see a doctor or other specified person. |
| Curator *ad litem* | Usually a lawyer | Court of Session or sheriff court | Power to carry on legal proceedings on behalf of person |

(adapted from McKay and Patrick, 1995, p. 103)

Case examples

1   An 84-year-old man who is housebound and who is a little confused at times but on the whole is alert and enjoys reading his daily newspaper.

2   A 68-year-old woman who has been diagnosed as being in the early stages of Alzheimer's disease.

3   A 32-year-old woman with severe learning difficulties who lives in a small group home but whose family is still very involved with her.

Comment

The above examples illustrate the range of situations in which someone might have to be appointed to take certain decisions on behalf of people unable to take them for themselves. Until April 2002, the law was unclear and fragmented in its approach. There were tutors-*dative* for welfare and/or financial decisions and curators *bonis* for financial decisions. Now a guardian can be appointed and the sheriff court will tailor the powers of a guardian to the needs of the adult. All guardians, including ones that have converted under the 2000 Act, must comply with the overarching principles in the Act. The Act also introduced an intervention order that may be sought from the sheriff court to deal with a specific situation that has arisen where a decision needs to be made on behalf of the adult with incapacity.

Adult with Incapacity Act 2000

In relation to the 84-year-old housebound man, while the benefit and least restrictive option principles of the Adults With Incapacity (Scotland) Act 2000 are relevant here it will also be important to work with this man to explore what he can and cannot do, what the concerns are and to think through what practical support he might need — for example he might want to make use of direct payments to buy in the help he needs at a particular time of the day. Similarly, in relation to the 68-year-old woman in the early stages of Alzheimer's disease, it might be very important for her to feel that she can exercise some control over the future and therefore she might want to consider, for example, making a continuing power of attorney in order to be confident that her financial affairs will be well looked after despite her deteriorating condition.

Some service users with acute support needs will have particular needs. Activity 12 provides you with an opportunity to explore this further in the context of dementia care in rural areas.

Allow about 1 hour

Website

Activity 12   Dementia care provision

Following the link from this activity on the course website, read the article by Innes et al. (2005) and make notes on the following questions:

1   Why is more knowledge required regarding service provision in rural areas for people with dementia?

2   What gaps in service provision are identified in the research and why is this important?

3   What were the positive aspects of dementia service provision for service users and carers?

4   What do you think were the key points made by the researchers in their conclusion?

Comment

According to the researchers there is a lack of information about dementia care generally and the experiences of people with dementia and their carers. Yet in Scotland there are over 58,000 people diagnosed as having dementia and with the projected increase in the number of older people in Scotland, more knowledge about services, how they are received and what is valued by service users and carers is important. The main gaps in service provision centred on transport, respite care, support for informal carers, home care and day care. However not all of these 'gaps' were the result of their rural location. One carer talked about wanting more home-based respite care – 'that would be best, that would mean there was almost no distress' (p. 358). There were clear messages about positive dementia care provision from service users and carers. For service users the appropriateness of the support was fundamental and both service users and carers valued the relationship between the service provider and the service user – a positive interpersonal relationship with the service provider is important. The main messages from the conclusion were the importance of informal local support networks, the 'discrepancy between the need for, and acceptance of, formal services' (in part explained by the desire to remain at home, concerns around privacy and guilt) and the value placed by service users and carers on being in control. The researchers conclude: 'services need to develop which are welcomed by service users and which reflect their perceptions of their care needs' (p. 363).

The concern, however, to ensure that a loved one is being properly cared for, which runs through much of the above discussions, is not the only issue. Dilemmas do not just centre on handling the understandable desire to protect. The neglect and abuse scandals that surface from time to time in relation to vulnerable older people should prompt all concerned – social work professionals, service users and carers – to place greater emphasis on the rights of older people and the need to respect their wishes and feelings. We turn to the issue of abuse and neglect next.

2.3 Protection from exploitation, abuse or harm

Abuse may be described as physical, sexual, psychological or financial. It may be intentional or unintentional or the result of neglect. It causes harm to the older person, either temporarily or over a period of time.

(Department of Health, 1993, p. 3)

The abuse or neglect of older people has never prompted the same kind of legislative response as the abuse or neglect of children; this despite there having been a similar pattern of serious incidents and local scandals. There is, of course, recourse available through both the civil and criminal law, using existing legislation. For example, an older person who can prove that a relative has stolen a valuable item from their home could have that person charged with theft. Similarly, an older person could seek recompense using the civil law for goods paid for but not received. However, there is not a systematic and recognised legislative route for dealing with such abuses of older people and, as with other vulnerable groups, achieving an appropriate standard of proof can be problematic.

In 2001 the Scottish Executive published a consultation paper looking at whether there was a need for legislation to protect all vulnerable adults. There was a high level of agreement with the proposals that the vulnerable adults provisions should be extended to groups other than persons with mental disorder and the possible introduction of provisions to exclude persons living with vulnerable adults, where the adult's health would be at risk. In 2006 the Adult Support and Protection (Scotland) Bill was introduced in the Scottish Parliament.

Box 21   The Adult Support and Protection (Scotland) Bill – main provisions

The Bill introduces measures to identify and protect adults at risk from abuse.

It defines adults at risk as adults who, because they are affected by disability, mental disorder, illness, infirmity or ageing, are:

- unable to protect themselves from abuse, or
- more vulnerable to being abused than persons who are not so affected.

Where it is known or suspected that an adult is being abused, it places a duty on councils to make the necessary enquiries to establish whether or not further action is required to stop or prevent abuse.

It introduces a general principle of intervention in an adult's affairs requiring action that is the least restrictive to the adult while providing benefit to him or her.

It introduces protection orders, which include assessment orders, removal orders and banning orders, all requiring approval by a sheriff.

It requires councils to set up adult protection committees to review procedures and practices of specified public bodies relating to the safeguarding of adults at risk.

[handwritten margin notes: See update. Adult Support + Protection bill (Scotland) 2007/2008.]

Even where the current legal framework could be used, however, there is often a reluctance to take legal action:

Griffiths *et al.* (1993) give three reasons for the current difficulties in implementing existing legislation. First, some legal procedures, particularly criminal prosecutions, are inappropriate in many cases of elder abuse because the perpetrators of the abuse are themselves victims of the situation (for example, carers subject to an excessive degree of stress). Second, legal procedures are often under-utilised because of negative attitudes/lack of expertise on the part of professionals such as lawyers and social workers. Third, the notion of abuse is seldom conceptualised in legal terms.

(Kingston and Penhale, 1995, pp. 198–9)

In Activity 13 you are asked to look more closely at the issues relating to older people and abuse.

Allow about 40 minutes

Reader

Activity 13   Abuse and the law

Read Chapter 13, 'Older people, abuse and the law', in the Reader and make notes on the following questions:

1   What do the authors say about the attitude to older people and how this affects the response to elder abuse?

2   What explanations are given for why elder abuse takes place?

Comment

The authors quote opinion that effective responses to elder abuse have to take into account and respond to negative attitudes and assumptions of ageism and marginalisation of older adults. To be old in many cultures and societies is to be reduced to the margins and to be regarded as increasingly frail, dependent and lacking in power. Powerlessness can become oppression and that can lead to abuse. Some of the relevant factors that are likely to lead to abuse are unrealistic expectations of carers, or carers who feel that they are forced to care even though they are unwilling to do so. Abuse does not only take place in the family home, it also takes place in institutional settings where, traditionally, staff have been unqualified or inexperienced, and the work has been seen as low status.

The protection of adults from abuse is not simply a question of whether or not to intervene or to involve the criminal justice system. It is also possible to use the Adults With Incapacity (Scotland) Act 2000 and mental health legislation to protect vulnerable adults.

> ### Box 22   Using the Adults With Incapacity (Scotland) Act 2000 and the Mental Health (Care and Treatment) (Scotland) Act 2003 to protect adults
>
> Two of the five principles that apply to this Act are that of 'minimum intervention' and 'taking into account the wishes of the adult'. While the Act itself is not focused directly on protecting adults from abuse, from April 2002 it introduced the possibility of investigation of alleged abuse. Any person can bring to the attention of the local authority any concerns about the welfare of an incapable adult. The local authority has a duty to investigate and the matter can be passed on for further investigation to the Mental Welfare Commission. Under the Act it is an offence for a person exercising powers such as guardianship to ill treat or neglect the person for whom they have responsibility.

> Under section 33 of the Mental Health (Care and Treatment) (Scotland) Act 2003 the local authority is under a duty to investigate if a person aged 16 years or over who has a mental disorder and is living in their area, 'may be, or may have been, subject, or exposed, at some place other than a hospital to ill-treatment, neglect or some other deficiency in care or treatment'.

Whistleblowing ↓.

The abuse of older people in residential care is a painful but continuing cause for concern. The Public Interest Disclosure Act 1998 made provision for employees to be able to speak out without fear of victimisation. The Act has a number of objectives, among which are to provide strong protection for workers who raise concerns internally and those who, for good reason, raise the concerns outside the organisation, for example, with the police.

> **Box 23   Disclosure**
>
> Disclosure is protected if one of the following appears to have occurred or is likely to occur and is being concealed:
> - a criminal offence
> - failure to comply with a legal obligation
> - a miscarriage of justice
> - a breach of health and safety
> - damage to the environment.

Whistleblowing

Organisations should have effective whistle-blowing procedures to ensure that no one is victimised for reporting concerns. You should also remember that a failure by a public authority to protect a person for whom they are responsible from inhuman or degrading treatment would be a breach of Article 3 of the European Convention on Human Rights (ECHR). A victim of such treatment, or someone acting on their behalf, could take action under the Human Rights Act 1998.

See update.

Care Inspectorate

Local authorities have clear responsibilities in the monitoring of care quality for older people in residential settings, through the intervention of individual social workers, despite the fact that registration and inspection is now the responsibility of the ~~Care Commission~~. Kingston and Penhale (1995, pp. 201–2) suggest the following guidelines for intervention in respect of abuse of older people in both domestic and residential settings:

- Workers should be encouraged to be vigilant about the possibility of abuse or neglect.
- Shared decision making is essential.
- Agencies need to develop policies which empower older people.
- The ultimate goal should be to ensure that older people enjoy a life which is free from violence and mistreatment.

Kitwood warns us of the depersonalising tendencies of some of those who work with elderly people with dementia. He refers to episodes that illustrate a 'malignant social psychology' (Kitwood, 1997, p. 46), although this does not necessarily suggest ill intent on the part of the care givers. Kitwood provides a long list of elements which contribute to this malignancy, including objectification, disempowerment, infantilisation, outpacing (for example, putting older people under pressure to do things more quickly than they can bear) and ignoring. He goes on to outline positive 'person work', identifying certain key processes for those working with people with dementia, including recognition, negotiation, play, celebration, validation and relaxation (Kitwood, 1997, pp. 90–1). However, concern about the quality of life of those who are unable to care for themselves is not confined to residential care. Action taken to enable the older person to live in their own community is also concerned with quality of life.

2.4 Alternative care

A residential home is an alternative when living in the community gets tough

At the beginning of this section you looked at the legislative options available when an older person is admitted to residential care in an emergency situation and against their wishes. Different legislative provisions are available where admission to residential care is the option of choice and takes place in a planned fashion. There are two forms of residential provision for older people which may involve social workers (although it should be noted that as a result of the Regulation of Care (Scotland) Act 2001 there are now no legal differences between residential and nursing homes and they are referred to as 'care homes').

Nursing home: the older person requires a degree of nursing care in addition to their social care needs. For example, they may be confined to bed at times and have health problems such as bedsores that require frequent medical attention. The staff of such units would include qualified nursing staff.

Residential home: while the older person may need to be looked after, this care is limited to their basic social and practical needs, such as provision of meals, help with bathing, assistance with dressing, and so on. While some staff may have a nursing background, there is no requirement for staff to be qualified nurses. Some care homes are registered to provide both basic and nursing care.

From April 2002 all of the above establishments had to be registered with the Scottish Commission for the Regulation of Care (the Care Commission) established by the Regulation of Care (Scotland) Act 2001. The Care Commission is responsible for registration, inspection and dealing with complaints. It should also be noted that it has regulatory responsibilities in relation to a wider range of services than just residential care and for other groups in addition to older people.

For social workers contemplating making use of powers of compulsion the legislation creates tensions: the desire to empower service users and provide them with maximum choice, while at the same time recognising the responsibility to protect the older person, perhaps even from themselves. Activity 14 explores the dilemmas involved in taking compulsory action to protect an older person from their own infirmity.

Allow about 40 minutes

Website

Activity 14   Compulsory care

Following the link from this activity on the course website, read the relevant Law Resource summaries and then look at the Miss Campbell case study below (you looked at this briefly in Section 1).

> Miss Campbell (81) lives alone in a two-room apartment on the third floor of a block of flats. She has angina and severe arthritis, which cause her to be confined to her home unless she has someone to accompany her. She currently receives the services of a home help for two hours twice a week, 'meals on wheels' three days a week and is visited every second Thursday by the district nurse, who baths her. Her niece, who is in regular employment, visits every evening and frequently stays overnight when Miss Campbell feels particularly distressed. Recently, Miss Campbell has become increasingly confused and on several occasions has allowed her sink to overflow, causing damage to her neighbour's ceiling.

See update.

Assume that you are the social worker and, having assessed her needs, you have decided that Miss Campbell would benefit from moving into residential care. What options would you have to help you to achieve this once you became aware of Miss Campbell's unwillingness to move out of her home?

Comment

Any decision to remove Miss Campbell compulsorily from her present home would not be taken lightly. It would be taken in the belief that it would be the best means of meeting her care needs. As the social worker, you would be aware of the research findings available (Cartwright, 1991) that suggest that such compulsory decisions create significant problems for older people's ability to settle into a new environment. Around 23 per cent die in the first year after admission.

(ASPA 07)
(SN SA)68 S. 132.A.

~~Section 47 of the National Assistance Act 1948~~ would enable the social worker, in conjunction with the designated medical officer of the health board, to arrange for Miss Campbell's transfer to hospital or some form of care home. It would be necessary to satisfy the conditions that she is incapable of caring for herself and that she is a danger to herself or others. The confusion and distress being experienced by Miss Campbell may well have had a serious effect on her ability to care for herself. The lapses of memory, which have caused her to allow her sink to overflow, could have serious implications for her downstairs neighbours.

If Miss Campbell's confusion and distress is diagnosed as dementia, it would be possible to either make use of the provisions of the Adults With Incapacity (Scotland) Act 2000, for example an order for guardianship – but remember the five principles apply – or, if the circumstances of the situation warranted it, invoke the powers

available under section 44 of the Mental Health (Care and Treatment) (Scotland)
Act 2003 to compulsorily admit her to hospital. If the situation was considered an
emergency, admission could take place under section 36 of the Mental Health (Care
and Treatment) (Scotland) Act 2003.

One of the difficulties of invoking these powers in respect of dementia
sufferers is that it is not always clear that 'treatment' is available. There
is some debate about whether hospital care and routine constitutes
'treatment'. You will look at mental health issues in more detail in
Section 4 of this block. Even if admission to hospital is necessary, it
remains important to adhere to core social work values such as
empowerment and treating service users with respect. Furthermore,
the decision to compulsorily remove someone from their home is a very
significant one which can have wide-ranging consequences. There are
concerns, for example, about the quality of life of older people admitted
to residential care homes and Cartwright's research (1991) into the lives
of older people in the last year of their lives outlines some of these
concerns. She observes that often friends and relatives thought
conditions in care homes were 'far from ideal' and cites Wilkin and
Hughes (1987) who argued that 'elderly people are often faced with a
choice between an unpleasant battle to survive in their own homes and
an equally unpleasant enforced dependence in the institution'.
Elsewhere in the article Cartwright paints a mixed picture of conditions
in care homes, with poor food, lack of mental stimulation and homes
not being equipped to meet the needs of those they were caring for. She
also writes that 'people take time to adjust' to living in residential
homes and cites the findings of Weaver and colleagues' research
(Weaver et al., 1985) which concluded that 'residents most able to come
to terms with admission were those who had exercised some degree of
control or choice in entering residential care'. In addition the inherent
vulnerability of older people must be taken into account alongside an
understanding of the power imbalance likely between residents and
staff in any residential setting. When you take into account anxieties
over costs, dependency and approaching death it is hardly surprising
that entry into care homes and the quality of life of those being cared
for is so contentious. Thus the regulation of care homes is increasingly
important – we turn to this next.

Registration and inspection

Social workers are unlikely to require a comprehensive understanding
of the legislation, regulations and guidance that apply in this area.
However, it is important that they understand the basic principles.

Registration covers such issues as maximum occupancy rates, age
range of occupants, level of care provided, quality standards, and so
on. A minimum standard will be specified below which the
establishment must not fall if it wishes to remain open.

Inspection is the process by which these standards are monitored. This
includes inspection of records as well as physical inspections of the
establishment on both a planned and unplanned basis. National Care
Standards were introduced in April 2002 to cover all service user
groups. They were developed by a consultative process which included
service users and carers. The standards have been developed from the
point of view of people who use the services and focus on quality of

life, rather than 'minimum' standards. These National Care Standards are made under authority from the Regulation of Care (Scotland) Act 2001 and are based on the principles in Box 24.

Box 24   National Care Standards – principles

The principles of the Standards are:

- dignity
- privacy
- choice
- safety
- realising potential
- equality and diversity.

The standards are addressed to the individual and are expressed in terms of rights, for example, in the National Care Standards for Care Homes for People With Learning Disabilities:

- You can keep control of your money and your personal belongings, unless your individual circumstances mean that specific legal arrangements have been made to look after them for you.
- You can see for yourself that your records are kept confidential and that access to them is only allowed in controlled circumstances.
- You do not have to stick to routines that fit in with staff.
- If you are capable of understanding that you need to take medication and what will happen if you do not do so, but you refuse to take it, staff must respect your wishes.

Activity 15 allows you to explore in more detail the role of the Scottish Commission for the Regulation of Care

---

Allow about 45 minutes

Audio CD

Activity 15   The Scottish Commission for the Regulation of Care

Listen to the interview with Annabel Fowles, head of legal services at the Scottish Commission for the Regulation of Care. Make notes on the following questions:

1   What is the role of the Care Commission?

2   What is the focus of the Care Commission inspection?

3   How does Annabel Fowles describe the relationship between the Care Commission and the service provider?

4   How easy is it to complain to the Care Commission?

5   Why are National Care Standards important?

Comment

The Care Commission was set up in April 2002 to regulate care services in Scotland; this includes care services from hospitals to childminders. There are a range of sanctions and powers available to the Scottish Commission for the Regulation of Care to enable it to improve services and to ensure a proper quality of service. Annabel Fowles refers to the emergency powers of the Care Commission as 'quite draconian'. The ultimate sanction is closure but the Care Commission emphasises improving services and to that end can issue condition and improvement notices in order to ensure compliance with the legislation. During inspections as much time as possible will be spent with service users and their representatives – the focus is on what service users think about the service. Thus at one level service users and carers are involved in commenting on and assuring the quality of service. Annabel Fowles sees the Care Commission as a critical friend for service providers – working with them to improve service delivery. Anyone can complain to the Care Commission – by phone or letter or via the web – any such complaints will be confidential. On completion of the investigation, complainants receive a resolution letter that outlines the complaint, how the investigation was carried out, the findings of fact, whether the complaint has been upheld and any action required on the part of the service provider. The National Care Standards are central to inspection and are guided by six principles (see Box 24). The National Care Standards are very accessible and can be very empowering for service users and carers in that they detail the rights of service users and the standards that must be complied with by service providers.

The National Care Standards are service-user focused – they have been developed from the point of view of people who use the services. They describe what each individual person can expect from the service provider. They focus on the quality of life that the person using the service actually experiences. Boxes 25 and 26 contain extracts from National Care Standards: Care Homes for Older People that illustrate their service user focus.

Box 25 Exercising your rights

Standard 10

You keep your rights as an individual.

1   You are confident that staff will treat you politely at all times and always respect your individuality.

2   Staff call you by your preferred name or title at all times.

3   If you need help, your request will be dealt with politely and as soon as possible.

4   Confidential information about you is only shared with others if you give permission, unless the law requires otherwise.

5   You will be told why any information cannot be kept confidential and who has the right to look at it.

6   You can be sure that your confidential records are held securely.

7   You know that any allegation of discrimination is properly investigated.

8   You are helped to understand your rights and responsibilities in relation to equal opportunities.

9   You are supported in keeping your civil rights (for example, in voting at elections)

Box 26 Expressing your views

Standard 11

You are encouraged to express your views on any aspects of the care home at any time.

1   You can freely discuss any concerns you have with your named worker, other residents or any member of the care home's management.

2   You know how to make a complaint or comment to the home about the service. You are also aware of the procedure for making formal complaints directly to the Commission.

3   The home deals with concerns and complaints quickly and sympathetically, and provides full information about what will happen as a result of the complaint.

4   You are encouraged and supported to use an independent and confidential advocacy service that can act for you. Staff will have information about any service that would help you in this way.

5   If you have an independent representative (for example, an independent advocate), staff will listen to what he or she has to say on your behalf, as if you were expressing the views yourself.

6   If you belong to an advocacy group, staff will take seriously suggestions or proposals that come from the group.

7   You can play a part in the Commission's inspection of your service.

8   The manager of your care home will make available a copy of each inspection report about the home so that you and your representative can look through it in your own time.

Funding

One of the most important changes created by the National Health Service and Community Care Act 1990 was to alter the funding arrangements for residential provision for older people. Before April 1993 any older person who was placed in a nursing home by the health board, usually following admission to hospital, would have the cost of their care met by the NHS. An older person who moved into residential care would have been expected to be assessed for a contribution towards their care. This anomaly has been addressed by the provisions for 'resource transfer' contained in the National Health Service Community Care Act 1990. This requires health boards to transfer to local authorities such funds as may be required to provide care for former hospital patients.

Any older person who is moved from hospital is now treated in the same way as if they were seeking admission to a residential home. Those of entirely independent means are assessed in terms of their suitability for the particular establishment. They will then meet the costs of care set by the establishment. Those who require the local authority to make a contribution towards the cost of their care need to have a community care assessment completed. As part of that assessment, a financial assessment is made to assess the person's ability to contribute to the cost of care.

This aspect of social work practice with older people raises many issues for social workers, who often find themselves cast in the role of 'rationer of resources'. It is often the case that a service user may be assessed as having a particular need, but the necessary funding or resources are not available. While social workers have a responsibility to record areas of unmet need on the community care assessment, this does not really acknowledge the depth of feeling experienced by workers operating within a system that cannot always respond to identified need. Having such a direct involvement in service users' financial affairs is often a new experience for social workers, who may find it awkward to explain to service users and their families that they are only likely to access particular services if they provide the funding themselves.

Section 22 of the National Assistance Act 1948 (as amended by the Community Care (Residential Accommodation) Act 1998) places a duty on local authorities to ensure that appropriate contributions towards the cost of care provision are collected. The exact formula applied in particular circumstances is complex and varies between authorities.

The charging thresholds as at April 2006 were £12,250 and £20,000, but there are no legal thresholds for home care services. If the person has capital below £12,250 it is ignored. If the person has between £12,250 and £20,000 they pay a proportion of the charge for residential care. If the person has over £20,000 they pay the full cost of residential care. There is provision in the Community Care and Health (Scotland) Act 2002 for thresholds for home care services, but these have yet to be introduced. The local authority can take legal steps to recover property given away or transferred at less than the real value, if it was deliberately disposed of to avoid charges for residential care. There is no time limit on how far back the local authority can look, but if the transfer was made in the six-month period before the service user entered residential care (or while in care), the local authority has the option to require the transferee to pay part of the charges, in addition to the normal option that applies to any transfer, that is, to treat the service user as if they still owned the property.

The service user's house is not always assessable. It will be disregarded if their spouse or partner, or a relative over 60 or under 16, or a relative who is incapacitated, carries on living there. There is a discretion to disregard the house if a person who gave up their own home to care for the service user carries on living there. If the house is assessable and charges remain unpaid, the local authority can attach a charging order on the house to secure the debt. Note that services may not be withdrawn if the service user refuses to pay as the provision of the service is separate from the collection of the debt.

The Community Care and Health (Scotland) Act 2002 makes provision for free personal and social care but not accommodation or living costs. Since 1 July 2002, personal care has been free to those aged 65 and over and nursing care (in a care home) has been free to anyone who needs it. There is still a charge for accommodation and food, subject to ability to pay. Charges for services should be made clear in any material produced and should be clearly explained to users as part of their assessment. The care plan should include a written explanation of any charges, and users should be advised of their rights to make representations.

In terms of the course themes, working in partnership, empowering service users, working with service users and carers and respecting their rights are central to work in this area. Working with diversity is also important given that alongside ageism, and the negative imagery and language associated with older people, there are issues of class, ethnicity and religion to be considered. The task of providing effective and valuable support in circumstances where there is considerable scope for misunderstanding and confusion is a very demanding one.

2.5 Conclusion

In this section you have looked at the range of powers and duties that the local authority has in relation to older people, whether they are living at home or in residential care. You have also considered the benefits of supporting older people so that they can continue to live independent lives in their own homes. In some circumstances that will not be possible.

The next section looks at the responsibilities of social workers in relation to people with disabilities.

Key points

- There is no special statute that provides for the promotion and safeguarding of the welfare of older people.
- There is a wide range of services that can be made available in order to support an older person in need staying in their own home.
- The Scottish Commission for the Regulation of Care has an important role to inspect and register residential services provided for older people and a wide range of other services.
- Providing appropriate care and support for older people and carers entails a commitment to working in partnership with them and listening to what they have to say.
- Workers need to be aware of and alert to the possibility of abuse of older people and other vulnerable service users in both domestic and residential settings.

3 Disability

For this section you need:

- course website access for online activities
- Reader, Chapters 10, 24 and 21.

Core questions

- What legislation applies specifically to people with disabilities?
- What are the roles and responsibilities of social workers in this field?
- How can social workers best support disabled service users and their carers?

3.1 Introduction

People with disabilities, such as people with physical, sensory and learning disabilities, are affected by the whole range of legislation that affects us all as citizens. However, in addition, there are specific laws whose aim is to enable people with disabilities to challenge and overcome discrimination and to access services in order to ensure that their quality of life is enhanced and that they are able to live their lives as fully participating members of society.

If you start from the premise that you can define the task of social work with people with disabilities as operating on the basis of partnership, this will mean ensuring that wherever possible the service user is fully involved in the decision-making processes that affect them. This should avoid the danger of being over-influenced by the medical model, which might regard the disability as a form of illness, and instead will allow a greater emphasis on issues of empowerment and rights and respecting the service-user perspective on their condition and situation. However, in order to ensure that rights are satisfied, social workers, people with disabilities and their carers need to know and understand the legislation, which bestows rights and imposes duties. In the introduction to this block, issues around social exclusion, stigma and the support needs of vulnerable adults were considered and recognised as impacting on the lives of, for example, disabled people. There is now specific legislation addressing negative discrimination experienced by disabled people as well as a duty to promote equality of opportunity for people with disabilities. There are also a number of statutes which are potentially relevant to service users and social work professionals. For example, section 12 of the Social Work (Scotland) Act 1968 imposes a duty on the local authority to promote social welfare by providing advice, guidance and assistance and services. In addition, because the definition of mental disorder in section 328 of the Mental Health (Care and Treatment) (Scotland) Act 2003 includes learning disability, the local authority duty under section 33 of that Act to investigate if someone is being or has been ill-treated or neglected includes people with learning disabilities, as does the right to independent advocacy contained in section 259 of the Act.

In addition it is important to remember that disabled people, like any service user group, now benefit from the added protection of the Human Rights Act 1998. The rights likely to be most relevant are:

Article 3 – protection from inhuman or degrading treatment

Article 5 – the right to liberty (e.g. care should be taken in relation to 'informal physical restraint' such as special chairs to prevent movement)

Article 6 – the right to a fair hearing (in order to participate effectively, the person may need an independent advocate)

Article 8 – the right to respect for private life.

The following sections deal separately with people with physical and learning disabilities. However, the issues facing social work professionals are similar. Working in partnership, knowledge of the legal framework and respecting the rights of service users and their carers are all essential to good and effective social work practice in this field.

3.2 People with physical disabilities

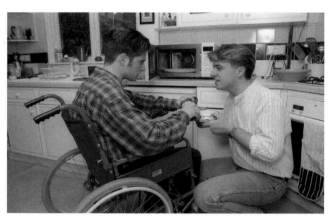

Local authorities have a duty to support people with physical disabilities

In Section 1 you were introduced to the range of legislation that addresses the needs of vulnerable people. This legislation is relevant to people with disabilities and the following activity will allow you to revisit it and explore its relevance to this group of service users.

Allow about 1 hour

Website

Activity 16   Working with disabled people

Following the link from this activity on the course website, read the Law Resource summaries and the following case study and make notes on the questions that follow.

> Mrs Gillespie, aged 50, had a stroke 12 months ago. As a result she has restricted movement on her right side, but has recovered her speech. The residual problems mean that she cannot walk unaided outside the house, cannot use the bath or shower without help, and basic household tasks are manageable but very difficult. Her husband left her some years ago and she and her 14-year-old daughter, June, live alone in their ground-floor flat. Mrs Gillespie used to work as a kitchen assistant at the local primary school and enjoyed her job. She now feels very isolated and that 'life is not really worth living. If it wasn't for June ...'

1   What is the relevant legislation affecting Mrs Gillespie and June?

2   What is the social work task in relation to this family?

Comment

Under section 12 of the Social Work (Scotland) Act 1968 the local authority is under a duty to provide advice, guidance and assistance to people in need. Mrs Gillespie is isolated – she may have need of services to help both with her emotional problems and with those caused by her disabilities. You should have identified the following statutory provisions as having a particular relevance for Mrs Gillespie and June:

1   Social Work (Scotland) Act 1968, section 12A (assessment of need for and provision of services). This might have been triggered by a referral from the doctor to the social work department when Mrs Gillespie was in hospital following her stroke.

2   Social Work (Scotland) Act 1968, section 12AA (request by carer for assessment of his or her ability to continue to provide care). However, she would also be entitled to an assessment under section 23 of the Children (Scotland) Act 1995 as a child affected by disability.

3   Social Work (Scotland) Act 1968, section 12A(4) (duty of the local authority to assess the need for services under section 2 of the Chronically Sick and Disabled Persons Act 1970). When making an assessment it would be obvious that Mrs Gillespie was suffering from a disability and therefore the social worker would have a clear duty to assess her need for such things as:

   • provision of a telephone

   • arranging for adaptations to secure her greater comfort or safety (for example, the installation of aids in the bathroom to help her to bathe independently)

   • provision of meals on wheels

   • provision of outings or other recreational facilities outside the home (very important considering Mrs Gillespie's isolation).

4   Social Work (Scotland) Act 1968, section 12B (direct payments in respect of community care services). A payment may have been made by the local authority to allow Mrs Gillespie to have choice in her care arrangements and to employ one or more people to assist her.

5   Social Work (Scotland) Act 1968, section 14 (provision of a home help, a need that may have been assessed in terms of section 12A).

As you have already seen, the Community Care and Health (Scotland) Act 2002 provides for an extended right to assessment for informal carers, including young carers. There is an independent right to request assessment that does not depend on whether the authority is also assessing the needs of the cared-for person.

As the social worker involved in this area of work, you would ensure that you are committed to principles of partnership and empowerment. Within this framework, you would have:

• assessed need

• provided appropriate services

• assessed risk

• maximised opportunities for independence.

You would have done this for both Mrs Gillespie and June.

Part of your role with Mrs Gillespie and June is defined by statute (for example, the duty to carry out a community care assessment). However, your assessment must be a holistic one and you will therefore have to take account of Mrs Gillespie's emotional state, her isolation, and June's need to be a 'normal' teenager and to get out to spend time with her friends. There is a danger that social workers might focus only on the disability and the needs that arise from it, and not respond to the service user as a whole person with a wide range of needs. You might, therefore, access counselling help for Mrs Gillespie if you are not able to provide it yourself.

Box 27 contains an extract from the Royal National Institute for the Blind (RNIB) (www) website on preparing for an assessment. It is useful both for service users and health and social care professionals.

Box 27   RNIB website advice on 'How can I prepare for the assessment?'

Before you meet the social services worker think carefully about any difficulties you are having and the kind of support you might need. This will help you – and the person doing the assessment – to make sure you cover everything.

You could think about the following areas:

- domestic tasks such as cleaning, cooking and shopping, learning to manage everyday tasks and advice about special equipment and how to make the best of any sight that you have
- getting around safely indoors and outdoors, advice about accommodation, including any adaptations your home might need to make it suitable for your needs – such as, improved lighting, guide rails, use of contrasting colours
- advice about communication – such as, using a computer keyboard or cassette recorder or learning braille
- getting a telephone
- meals at home or at a suitable centre, perhaps a luncheon club
- personal care – such as, bathing, cutting your toenails, getting up and going to bed
- advice about your financial affairs – such as, benefits, and making ends meet
- advice about your leisure and employment choices
- advice about taking a break, either for you or for someone looking after you
- social work support and advice
- adjusting to your disability, counselling or talking over any personal problems
- help with transport to and from services.

In addition to the above obligations on local authorities to take steps to support those who are disabled, the Disability Discrimination Act 1995 outlaws discrimination against people with disabilities in employment, the provision of goods and services, and access to services. Social workers may also have an advocacy role in relation to disabled people: for example, advocating on their behalf to make sure that they can access a particular service by arguing for its relocation to a more appropriate venue. There may also be a need for independent advocacy if the social worker has a conflict of interest in trying to empower the service user while operating within a local authority with limited resources. Activity 17 asks you to look more closely at the Disability Discrimination Act 1995 and other legislation affecting disabled people.

Allow about 40 minutes

Activity 17 Disability and the law

Reader

Read Chapter 10, 'Disability and the law', in the Reader and make notes on the following questions:

1 Why does the author say that there is a lack of understanding surrounding the term 'disability'?

2 What is the definition of disabled in the Disability Discrimination Act 1995?

3 Does the fact that a person is disabled within the meaning of the Act guarantee them the protection of the Act?

4 What is the definition of disabled in the Chronically Sick and Disabled Persons Act 1970?

Comment

There are varying definitions of disability in legislation, which means that there may be a lack of clarity in people's minds about what is meant by 'disability' or 'disabled'. The definition in the 1995 Act 'is a person who has a physical or mental impairment which has a substantial and long term adverse effect on his ability to carry out normal day-to-day activities'. This is a complex definition and means that simply showing that you have a disability is not sufficient to gain the protection of the Act. You must also show that your physical or mental impairment has a substantial and long-term adverse effect on your ability to carry out normal day-to-day activities. These activities are also defined in the Act and do not include the ability to work, so it may be argued that they do not fully cover all normal day-to-day activities. The definition of disabled in the 1970 Act is shorter: 'chronically sick or disabled or suffering from a mental disorder'. Apart from the term 'mental disorder', which is now defined in the Mental Health (Care and Treatment) (Scotland) Act 2003, the other terms are open to interpretation. The duty to promote equality of opportunity under the Disability Discrimination Act 1995 came into force in December 2006. The extent of this duty is summarised in Box 28.

TMALY (handwritten annotation)

See update! (handwritten annotation)

> ### Box 28 Duty to promote equality for disabled people
>
> The Disability Discrimination Act 2005 sets out a general duty which requires every public authority in carrying out its functions to have due regard to:
>
> - the need to eliminate discrimination that is unlawful under the Act
> - the need to eliminate harassment of disabled persons that is related to their disability
> - the need to promote equality of opportunity between disabled persons and other persons
> - the need to take steps to take account of disabled persons' disabilities, even where that involves treating disabled people more favourably than other persons
> - the need to promote positive attitudes towards disabled persons
> - the need to encourage participation by disabled persons in public life

The Disability Discrimination (Public Authorities) (Statutory Duties) (Scotland) Regulations 2005 set out specific steps that specified bodies must take to fulfil the general duty, including a duty to:

- publish a Disability Equality Scheme demonstrating how it intends to fulfil its general and specific duties
- involve disabled people in the development of the scheme
- carry out impact assessments
- make arrangements for gathering relevant information;
- develop an 'action plan'
- take the steps set out in its action plan, within three years
- publish a report.

See update.

A statutory Code of Practice, produced by the Disability Rights Commission (DRC, 2005), provides practical advice on what the duty means and how public authorities can meet their obligations. It is available on the Disability Rights Commission's website (www).

3.3 People with learning disabilities

In this area of work, partnership is again a theme – partnership with service users and with carers. Where service users have carers, both the service user and the carer need to be consulted about the assessment of their needs, and their concerns need to be addressed in jointly devised strategies. Partnership may also extend to working with other agencies in the assessment and provision of services.

In addition to the assessment of need and the provision of services, social work with people with learning disabilities might include:

- promotion of employment opportunities
- promotion of education and leisure opportunities
- development of independence and life skills
- advocacy.

Box 29   Relevant legislation

The legislation in respect of community care has relevance to people with learning disabilities because they are regarded as being 'persons in need' (section 94 of the Social Work (Scotland) Act 1968).

Mental Health (Care and Treatment) (Scotland) Act 2003

The local authority has further specific duties in relation to this group of service users:

Section 25 – to provide care and support services
Section 26 – to provide services designed to promote well-being and social development
Section 27 – to provide assistance with travel.

These duties can be fulfilled by the provision of resource centres or day centres, which can be funded by the local authority or delivered in partnership with a voluntary agency. It can also involve the social work department in facilitating attendance at a college or training course.

Adults With Incapacity (Scotland) Act 2000

Guardianship under this Act may be required for some people with learning disabilities who are unable to make decisions for themselves. The local authority has a duty to apply for welfare guardianship if it appears to be necessary and there is no one willing or able to apply.

In May 2000 the Scottish Executive (2000b) published the report *The same as you? A review of services for people with learning disabilities.*

The main aims outlined in the report were as follows:

- The main aim is for people with learning disabilities to be included – in community life, in education, in leisure and recreation and in employment. They should also have far greater access to *mainstream* services and rely less on specialist services.

- To achieve these goals there is a need to improve, reshape and reorganise services, and the public needs to better understand people with learning disabilities and their needs.

- At the centre of this is a major shift to person-centred and needs-led approaches, which put the individual at the heart of any decisions made. For that to work, people with learning disabilities need better information to make more informed choices, to be supported by an advocate if they want, and to have more control over their lives and services.

- Local area coordinators will replace care managers and care management and will:

  – coordinate and arrange support and services

  – act as a voice for people with learning disabilities

  – have a budget to buy new, local and cost-effective services.

- Every person who wants to have one should have a 'personal life plan'.

- The balance of care needs to shift. Very few people should have hospital as their home, and other forms of shared living should reduce. Day services have to modernise and focus more on education, employment and personal fulfilment and there needs to be more support for carers.

- People with learning disabilities, their carers and providers need someone to act for them and promote a better general understanding of learning disabilities. The Scottish Consortium for Learning Disability will do this by being a centre of excellence, providing leadership to agencies in the field and advice in general.

- To serve people with learning disabilities better, agencies need to be much clearer about their roles and the opportunities for working with others (particularly for people with extra and *complex needs*). There needs to be effective partnerships between agencies, between professionals, and between users, carers and professionals.

- The public should be helped generally to be more aware and understanding of learning disabilities through an ongoing programme of awareness.

- Practice and progress should be monitored to make sure that the changes take place and are developed and maintained.

Implementation of these recommendations is now underway as follows.

- The first agreements for Partnerships in Practice were in place in 2001. They aim to provide a clear focus within local authority and health planning systems on agencies working together to develop services for people with learning disabilities.

- Training for local coordinators began in late 2001.

- The Scottish Executive has distributed change funds to help local authorities implement the changes.

- There have been changes to make direct payments more accessible.

People with learning disabilities should enjoy recreation and leisure

To keep up to date with further progress you can go to the Scottish Executive website (www) for the national Review of Services for People with a Learning Disability.

People with learning disabilities can be very vulnerable. In 2004 the Social Work Services Inspectorate/Mental Welfare Commission Scottish Borders Inquiry prompted the setting up of the 21st Century Social Work review and new legislation imposing a duty on social workers to investigate and prevent the abuse of adults (SWSI/MWC, 2004). Box 30 summarises the facts of the Social Work Services Inspectorate Scottish Borders Inquiry and highlights some of the key findings.

Box 30   Scottish Borders Inquiry

Summary of the facts

In March 2002 a woman was admitted to Borders General Hospital after she had gone to the house of a friend who found her to be badly injured and called an ambulance. She was taken to hospital with multiple injuries from physical and sexual assault. A police investigation revealed a catalogue of abuse and assaults over the previous weeks and possibly much longer. Three men were convicted of the assaults later in 2002.

The woman was considered to have a learning disability. A series of events had led to her being cared for by one of the convicted offenders. Over many years, there were events and statements in records held by social work, health services and the police that raised serious concerns about this person's behaviour toward this woman.

Other individuals were receiving care under the same circumstances. They had varying degrees of learning disabilities, physical disabilities and mental health needs, which were largely neglected, to the point of becoming potentially life-threatening for some. Health and social work records contained numerous statements of concern about their care, including allegations of serious abuse and exploitation that were not acted upon. From late 2000, the lives of these individuals became increasingly chaotic. They were neglected, lived in unsuitable and unsanitary conditions and were financially and sexually exploited.

Findings
The inquiry found a:

- failure to investigate appropriately very serious allegations of abuse
- lack of comprehensive needs assessments
- lack of information-sharing
- lack of care plans
- lack of understanding of the legislative framework for intervention and its capacity to provide protection
- failure to consider statutory intervention at appropriate stages
- failure to understand and balance the issues of self-determination and protection
- failure to protect the finances of vulnerable individuals
- lack of understanding of the complexities of child/adult protection and of the need to explore all allegations of abuse and the possible reasons for retraction of these
- failure to communicate with service users or to engage them effectively in assessing their needs.

Overall these failings emphasised the importance of joint working.

This inquiry highlighted how the vulnerability of people with learning disabilities could be compounded by the failure of adult professionals to take them seriously and a lack of professionalism. The Adults With Incapacity (Scotland) Act 2000 has raised awareness among families of adults with learning disabilities of the possibility of guardianship as a means of making arrangements whereby stable and continuous management of a person's financial and welfare interests can be put in

place. There has been a significant increase since 2002. In the year 2004/2005 there were 531 cases of guardianship (Mental Welfare Commission for Scotland, 2006).

The Mental Welfare Commission (MWC) also monitors the operation of the rules governing compulsory treatment. Situations can arise where someone suffering from severe learning disabilities requires physical treatment for which they cannot give consent. The MWC gives guidance to physicians on how they might deal with such cases. It noted in its Annual Report 1997–8:

> There is an increasing tendency towards caution among physicians, surgeons and others when contemplating treatment which might be risky, irreversible, contentious or not reasonably likely to succeed. The problem is that this caution could lead to incapable adults being deprived of treatment which could potentially relieve suffering or greatly enhance the quality of life.
>
> (Mental Welfare Commission for Scotland, 1998, p. 56)

Treatment not covered by the Mental Health (Care and Treatment) (Scotland) Act 2003 requires the usual consent. This means that either the patient must consent (many detained patients would be able to consent to medical treatment) or a person who is legally appointed to the patient for this purpose must consent. This could be a welfare guardian or a welfare attorney under the Adults With Incapacity (Scotland) Act 2000. If the patient cannot consent and there is no one legally appointed, doctors can treat the patient without consent, using a procedure under the Adults With Incapacity (Scotland) Act 2000 whereby they must certify incapacity and explain why the treatment will benefit the patient: this is done on prescribed forms. Activity 18 asks you to look at the work of the voluntary organisation Enable, which campaigns for improvements in opportunities for people with learning disabilities and their families by developing and providing services that support people to live, work and enjoy a meaningful role in everyday life.

See update.

Allow about 30 minutes

Activity 18   Enable

Reader

Read Chapter 24, 'Enable', in the Reader and answer the following questions:

1   What sort of work is Enable involved in?

2   Why do you think there is a need for Enable Legal Services?

Comment

Enable is the largest national voluntary organisation for people with learning disabilities and their families and carers in Scotland. It provides a range of services such as supported employment, small care homes, supported living services, community day care services, short breaks and out of school care for children. It also provides a Legal and Information Advice Service and campaigns on behalf of people with learning disabilities and their carers. Enable Legal Services is needed because this area of law is very specialist. It is not taught in any depth in law degree courses and many firms of solicitors would not have someone with this sort of specialist knowledge. Clients may also feel more comfortable accessing advice through a charitable organisation than through a firm of solicitors. They may also worry about the cost of accessing advice through a firm of solicitors.

Activity 19 gives you the opportunity to consider the knowledge, skills and values a social worker might need to call on when undertaking work with a young person with learning disabilities and their family.

Allow about 20 minutes

Activity 19   Planning for the future

Read the case below and make notes on what you consider would need to be covered in any assessment for Fiona.

Fiona is a 15-year-old girl with Down's syndrome. She lives with her parents and 19-year-old brother. She has attended mainstream secondary school, where she has been happy, although her parents constantly worry about her and are rather over-protective. Her friends at school are talking of going to college when they leave school and Fiona has said that she would like to do this too. This will involve her travelling by bus into the centre of town and her parents are not happy about this. You are asked by the education department to complete an assessment for Fiona. Her parents have not had any contact with the social work department.

Comment

The assessment for Fiona would need to cover such matters as her continuing education, her consequent transport requirements, and other support she might need in order to be able to take advantage of the educational opportunity. In this case Fiona is able to state clearly what her wishes are and we can assume that with help and support she can make a decision about what she would like to happen to her after she leaves school. At the same time her parents have not had any contact with the social work department. Perhaps they have deliberately avoided contact because they mistrust social workers. Work with Fiona and her parents will have to be sensitive to their ideas about what they want to happen as well as their possible suspicion of outsiders getting involved in family matters.

One of the difficulties faced by the social worker in this case is the complexity it presents in terms of responding to the different and potentially competing demands within the family. The knowledge, skills and values that are relevant to the social worker in this case would be:

- knowledge of theory related to aspects of learning disability and family functioning; knowledge of agency procedures and resources; knowledge of the legislation

- skills in assessment, advocacy and empowerment

- values – the Scottish Social Services Council requirements are relevant here. The social worker will have to consider the right of choice that both Fiona and her parents have. He or she will have to balance the need to protect Fiona with trying to assist her to increase control over, and improve the quality of, her life. There is also the dilemma of responding to the competing demands of Fiona and her parents.

Family carers of people with learning disabilities often have fears about what will happen in the future when the carer dies or becomes too frail to continue to provide care. Research shows (Walker and Walker, 1998) that family carers are often reluctant to seek help because of previous negative experiences and a fear that by doing so they may be admitting to their own diminishing competence and will thus lose control. The task of completing an assessment of future needs may be an invaluable opportunity to begin to build up a partnership based on trust with the carers and the person with learning disabilities, one which can be used in the future either to respond to crises or to plan positively. A social worker might also have to face the situation where relatives disagree with their professional opinion about the capacity of an adult to decide on a particular matter or purport to speak for the adult when he or she is able to speak for themselves. One way to deal with such situations is to introduce the adult to an independent advocate. Some advocacy services will also provide a second advocate for relatives. Independent advocates either act in accordance with the views and wishes of the adult, or, if the adult has difficulty in expressing his or her views and wishes, the advocate will attempt to assess what might be in the interests of the adult, but free from professional and resource constraints. An independent advocate is not there to help other professionals to achieve what they want, rather to make sure that the views and wishes of the adult are properly represented, either by the adult themselves or, if they prefer, by the advocate. The presence of an independent advocate can be very empowering for service users, particularly in relation to effective participation at meetings. It can help to address the power imbalance between service user and professionals and empower the service user to take more control over their life. You should bear in mind that not all areas in Scotland have access to an independent advocacy service and that even where there is a service, it may have a waiting list, due to limited resources.

Activity 20 asks you to look at the work of an independent advocacy service.

Allow about 30 minutes

Activity 20   Independent advocacy

Reader

Read Chapter 21, 'Independent advocacy: a practice perspective', in the Reader and answer the following questions:

1   What are the three key features of independent advocacy?

2   Why is independent advocacy needed?

3   How might professionals react to independent advocacy?

Comment

The three key features of independent advocacy are:

- independence
- absence of conflicts of interest
- advocates not having 'professional' views.

It should be clear from this list that it is not possible for professionals who provide other services to also provide independent advocacy.

Independent advocacy is needed because many service users find it hard to express their views or challenge professional decisions. This is because there can be a power imbalance between the service user and the professional and also because service users often lack the confidence to speak out. An advocate can help them to overcome these barriers. Professionals can feel threatened by independent advocates and may feel that they are being personally criticised or that the involvement of an advocate reflects badly on their practice or their relationship with the service user. In addition some people cannot communicate verbally – they too will require the support of an independent advocate if their wishes and feelings are to be given proper consideration.

Professionals who understand and accept the need for independent advocacy are demonstrating to service users that their views are important and that it is acceptable to comment on or even criticise services and to ask for change. This is in keeping with the concept of empowerment. It is now accepted that the role of advocates and supporters is essential in making sure that the views of disabled people are heard and their rights are respected. Indeed, section 259 of the Mental Health (Care and Treatment) (Scotland) Act 2003 provides that every person with a mental disorder, which includes people with learning disabilities, 'shall have a right of access to independent advocacy' and imposes a duty on local authorities and health boards to secure the availability of independent advocacy services and service user access to such services.

3.4 Conclusion

Social work in relation to disabled people calls for the use of a range of skills and a commitment to empowering practice. The challenge of this area revolves around not just the need to work with service users who may have complex support requirements but also the need to work with the disabled person's carer and family, while recognising that the relatives may not have any legal right to make decisions on behalf of the service user, unless they have been formally appointed to do so. Furthermore service users and their families need to be clear that there is a substantial difference between the right to have a view taken into account and the right to make legal decisions.

Key points

- In addition to general community care legislation there is specific legislation covering people with disabilities.
- There are a number of professionals with particular tasks and responsibilities in relation to those with a learning disability.
- The social work task in relation to people with disabilities is highly skilled and rests on established principles of good practice.
- All work with people with disabilities must pay proper regard to their carers and family and take place in partnership with them.
- All work with people with disabilities must pay proper regard to the person's right to self-determination and choice.

4 Mental health

For this section you need:

- audio CD
- course website access for online activities
- Reader, Chapter 6.

Core questions

- What are the key provisions of the Mental Health (Care and Treatment) (Scotland) Act 2003?
- What are the principles underpinning the Mental Health (Care and Treatment) (Scotland) Act 2003?
- What is the meaning of mental disorder?
- What are the roles and responsibilities of the mental health officer (MHO) under the Mental Health (Care and Treatment) (Scotland) Act 2003?
- What are advance statements and why are they important?
- On what grounds can guardianship under the Adults with Incapacity (Scotland) Act 2000 be acquired?
- What are the powers and remit of the Mental Health Tribunal for Scotland?
- What is the role of the Mental Welfare Commission (MWC)?

4.1 Introduction

This section provides an overview of mental health legislation in Scotland and the social work role in this area. It introduces the key principles and processes underpinning the legal framework and will enable you to understand the mandate for social work practice in this specialist field. It is beyond the scope of this course to consider in detail the provisions of mental health law. (Social work students wishing to become mental health officers have to undertake post-qualifying education in this subject, see Section 4.3).

Before it is possible to consider the legal context it is necessary to acknowledge that public perceptions of mental health continue to affect social work practice. There are different understandings of what mental health is and what it means to have mental health needs. The term is often used to refer to mental illness or mental disorder and their treatment, where mental illness is a diagnosable condition that significantly interferes with an individual's cognitive, emotional or social abilities At other times the term mental health is used in a more positive way to convey the idea of mental well-being, including issues as diverse as being optimistic, having high self-esteem, and a sense of belonging.

Many of us can be seen as having mental heath needs at some point in our lives, as Box 31 illustrates.

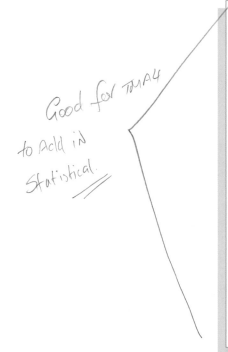

Good for ??? ???
to Add in
Statistical.

Box 31   Incidence of mental health needs

Estimates of the prevalence of mental distress in Britain vary. The Office for National Statistics (ONS) puts the figure at one in six adults at any one time. Another major survey that is frequently quoted puts the figure at one in four. The one in six figure represents those people defined as having 'significant' mental health problems, while the latter survey uses a wider definition of mental health problems. This also includes a breakdown of the progress that these one in four people are likely to make through the mental health system as follows:

- around 300 out of every 1,000 people will experience mental health problems every year in Britain
- 230 of these will visit a general practitioner (GP)
- 102 of these will be diagnosed as having a mental health problem
- 24 of these will be referred to a specialist psychiatric service
- 6 will become inpatients in psychiatric hospitals.

(MIND, 2005)

According to MIND (www) one in four of us will have mental health needs at some point in our lives, though an open public discussion of this is hindered by the serious stigma attached to those perceived as being mentally ill. In Section 1 of this block you considered the prejudicial attitudes that people with mental health needs face in everyday life. This makes the flavour of some of the contemporary comment and debate on mental health problematic. If a need for mental health services is seen as something that can affect any of us, for example due to divorce or bereavement, the public conversation on mental health issues would be different, as would be the demands made of services and mental health professionals.

Recent debates around mental health have been complex and intense. One reason for this is the emergence of a risk and dangerousness agenda – an agenda fuelled by the anxiety surrounding high-profile cases where people with acute mental health needs have committed a serious criminal offence, having been either discharged from hospital or not provided with appropriate and effective supervision in the community (see Box 32).

Box 32   The killing of Jonathan Zito

Jonathan Zito was killed by Christopher Clunis in 1992. Jonathan was with his brother at Finsbury Park underground station when Clunis approached him from behind and fatally stabbed him in the eye. He had been married for just three months to Jayne Zito. Christopher Clunis suffered from schizophrenia. The report into Jonathan Zito's killing revealed a catalogue of errors and missed opportunities in Clunis's care, stretching back over many years. He had a long history of violence, institutional care and non-compliance with treatment programmes.

In Scotland the MWC inquiry into Mr L and Mr M (see Box 33) revealed poor risk management and communication and a failure to provide proper supervision on discharge.

INTERESTING

Box 33   MWC Inquiry into the care and treatment of Mr L

Mr L was a restricted patient on conditional discharge living in the community when he murdered Mr M. The inquiry identified weaknesses in the management of risk by the professional staff providing care and supervision and made particular recommendations for all agencies involved, including social work.

One of the recommendations of the report is that social workers supervising conditionally discharged patients must be MHOs. The social work department must ensure that these social workers have the necessary competences and training to carry out their supervisory function. The inquiry recommended that MHOs supervising conditionally discharged patients have regular supervision from another member of staff who has experience of working with high-risk patients.

These debates have resulted in calls for the extension of legal powers of intervention and control, in order to protect the public. For example the Mental Health (Care and Treatment) (Scotland) Act 2003 allows for compulsory powers of treatment in the community.

Good for TMA 4

However, there is another aspect to recent policy concerns and one which is reflected in the provisions of the Mental Health (Care and Treatment) (Scotland) Act 2003 – an increased demand for service users' rights to counterbalance what is perceived by some as the excessive power of mental health professionals. The Mental Health (Care and Treatment) (Scotland) Act 2003 provides new substantive and procedural rights to service users and their families that will be considered in the next section.

Historically, social work practice in this field can be characterised as paternalistic, one in which those working with people with mental disorder are concerned to support them and alleviate their condition. In 2004 a *British Medical Journal* (BMJ) editorial on the Mental Health (Care and Treatment) (Scotland) Act 2003 stated that:

> The ethical basis for mental health legislation has developed from paternalism, emphasising dangerousness and humane care, towards autonomy, emphasising individual rights and capacity. Autonomy features prominently in the new act ... In Scotland concern remains about resources, bureaucracy, implementation, and training.
>
> (BMJ, 2004, p. 634)

The editorial nonetheless concludes that 'Scotland will have ethically sound modern legislation, with principles supported by most stakeholders' (BMJ, 2004).

So what does this mean? Later the BMJ editorial observed:

> The introduction of the Mental Health Tribunal for Scotland marks a major change in the legal review process. Extra safeguards and supports should be provided by advocacy services, the recognition of advance statements, an extended role for the Mental Welfare Commission for Scotland, and the introduction of named people.
>
> (BMJ, 2004, pp. 634–5)

Thus policy and practice debates on mental health matters have in recent years been concerned with risk, dangerousness, service users' rights as well as the use and abuse of professional power. These concerns, however, have not always received equal coverage in public media debates about mental illness and are reflected in competing demands that create dilemmas for practice.

Many people who have mental health problems seek treatment as outpatients or inpatients, or receive help from voluntary organisations or social work departments, and might have little knowledge of the law or their rights as the user of mental health services. In this respect they are in much the same position as anyone else receiving help from the health services and social work departments. However, for some people with mental health needs the law is very important.

[handwritten note: Some considerations the SW must be aware of in relation to public perception]

The law and social work practice in relation to mental health can give rise to important human rights issues. One reason for this is that MHOs can be involved in the process of depriving people of their liberty. This 'coercive' aspect of mental health law is significant. The Mental Health (Care and Treatment) (Scotland) Act 2003 provides for three forms of compulsion – short-term detention, emergency detention and applications to the mental health tribunal for a compulsory treatment order. These powers are in stark contrast to the legal position of patients with physical illnesses, who retain the right to refuse treatment in most circumstances.

Activity 21 begins to explore the range of situations in which people might have need of mental health services and why the law is important.

Allow about 20 minutes

Activity 21   Receiving mental health services

[handwritten note: lack of Capacity – Need to Safeguard Person from Self + others. Temporary breakdown – preserve what they have + provide support to cope]

Identify two situations in which you think the law could be important to people receiving mental health services and explain why this might be so.

Comment

One situation that is more common than many might realise is where a person finds themselves unable to cope (due to work pressure or a domestic crisis) – they might be in need of mental health services in the form of counselling. This would probably be a genuinely voluntary choice. However, there are circumstances in which people with mental health needs can find themselves that can involve the possibility of a reduction in their freedom and civil liberties; for example where a person with severe depression is feeling suicidal and they are detained in hospital for their own good. The law then becomes a way of safeguarding a particularly vulnerable group of people. It is important that social workers understand not only their duties and powers under the Mental Health (Care and Treatment) (Scotland) Act 2003 but also the legal safeguards that exist to protect people who are suffering from mental disorders.

Because of a mental disorder, a person may be:

- compulsorily detained in hospital

- made subject to compulsory treatment

- unable to give consent to valid treatment

- in need of help to manage their finances and property

- in need of legal protection of their rights during any period of compulsory hospitalisation

- in need of support in performing day-to-day activities.

Many people are unable to cope

Good definition of Mental Health.

In law the term 'mental disorder' has a particular meaning. Under section 328 of the Mental Health (Care and Treatment) (Scotland) Act 2003 mental disorder is defined as meaning any 'mental illness, personality disorder, or learning disability'. It is thus wide in scope and for the remainder of this block any reference to mental disorder is within the meaning of section 328 of the Mental Health (Care and Treatment) (Scotland) Act 2003. Section 4.1 has briefly outlined the potential relevance of law as a safeguard of service users' interests and rights; Section 4.2 will provide you with an opportunity to become familiar with the key provisions of the Mental Health (Care and Treatment) (Scotland) Act 2003.

4.2 The legal framework

There are three statutes that are relevant in the field of mental health. Section 12 of the Social Work (Scotland) Act 1968 provides for local authority support for service users in need. Furthermore, as you will have seen in earlier sections of this block, under section 13A of the Social Work (Scotland) Act 1968 the local authority is under a duty 'to arrange residential accommodation with nursing provision if it appears necessary for a person due to infirmity, age, illness or mental disorder...'. Second, there is the Mental Health (Care and Treatment) (Scotland) Act 2003, which came into force in October 2005. Finally, there are the guardianship and intervention provisions of the Adults With Incapacity (Scotland) Act 2000, which you examined in Section 3 of this block. According to the MWC's Annual Report for 2005–2006 there has been 'a rise in the proportion of guardianships being sought

Key Point re Guardianship

MWC – mental Welfare Commission

for people with dementia. More local authorities may be using guardianship to move people with dementia to care homes because of legal advice' (MWC, 2006, p. 82). The reasoning here is that this avoids delay and such delay 'may impair the adult's ability to manage many aspects of their care for themselves ... [and] in many cases ... does not seem to serve any benefit to the adult' (MWC, 2006, pp. 82–83). There are thus a number of overlapping statutory provisions that are important in the field of mental health (see generally McManus and Thomson, 2005). As we have explored in some detail the Social Work (Scotland) Act 1968 and Adults With Incapacity (Scotland) Act 2000 in earlier sections, here we focus on the Mental Health (Care and Treatment) (Scotland) Act 2003.

The Mental Health (Care and Treatment) (Scotland) Act 2003 is the first major change in the legislation since 1984. The 1984 Act reflected the then current situation, which was that most people with chronic or acute mental illnesses were still cared for in hospital. While people with acute illnesses will still be hospitalised, a large number of people classed as suffering from mental disorders now live in the community.

In October 2001, following on from the report by the Millan Committee, which was set up to review mental health law in Scotland and make proposals for reform, the Scottish Executive published a policy statement called *Renewing Mental Health Law* (Scottish Executive, 2001b). This set out the Executive's plans for major changes to mental health law. It came into force in October 2005 and replaced the Mental Health (Scotland) Act 1984.

The Mental Health (Care and Treatment) (Scotland) Act 2003 places an emphasis on treatment in the community and detention in hospital may only be used if it is the most appropriate and least restrictive way of dealing with the patient. The Act also gives a legal right to an independent advocate to any person with a mental disorder and it contains a list of principles which must be followed by anyone exercising functions under the Act. Activity 22 provides an opportunity to consider the main provisions and rationale for the Mental Health (Care and Treatment) (Scotland) Act 2003

Allow about 1 hour

Reader

Activity 22   Mental health and social work

Read Chapter 6, 'Mental health and social work', in the Reader and answer the following questions:

1   To what extent have service users been involved in mental health discussion and debate?

2   What are the main changes in the Mental Health (Care and Treatment) (Scotland) Act 2003 (referred to in the chapter as the Mental Health Bill)?

3   What opportunity does the author think that the Act presents to social workers?

Comment

Service users became more involved in mental health discussion and debate during the 1990s, although their involvement was still sometimes tokenistic and patchy. No service users were involved in the preparation of the legislation in the 1980s, but by contrast there was considerable service user involvement in the Millan Committee Report, which preceded the 2003 Act.

see update

The main changes introduced in the Act are:

- a set of underpinning principles
- the introduction of a Mental Health Tribunal for Scotland to replace the role of the sheriff court
- new duties on local authorities to promote the health and well-being of people with mental health problems living in the community
- the possibility of being admitted directly for short-term detention, rather than via emergency detention
- compulsory treatment orders to allow for treatment in the community as an alternative to detention
- a prohibition on electro-convulsive therapy (ECT) if the patient is competent to refuse
- the replacement of the 'nearest relative' with a 'named person' chosen by the patient
- the right to an independent advocate
- the right to make an advance statement about treatment and to have it taken into account.

Ferguson sees the Mental Health (Care and Treatment)(Scotland) Act 2003 as presenting an opportunity for social workers to develop genuinely anti-oppressive practice in mental health. This legislation can be seen as securing effective care and treatment by:

- ensuring that emergency, short-term and longer-term periods of detention in hospital may only take place where strict criteria have been met and where clearly defined procedures have been followed
- establishing the Mental Health Tribunal for Scotland to make decisions in relation to compulsory measures
- strengthening patients' rights
- giving the MWC and the patient's responsible medical officer the right to refer a compulsory treatment order to the mental health tribunal for review
- giving powers to the Mental Health Tribunal for Scotland to make major decisions affecting the management of restricted patients, such as discharge for patients on a restriction order and compulsion order, and, for patients subject to hospital directions or transfer for treatment directions, the power to direct the Scottish ministers to cancel these directions.

The Mental Health (Care and Treatment) (Scotland) Act 2003 thus defines the nature, duties and powers of the key organisations, for example the Mental Health Tribunal for Scotland, and individuals within the legal framework, for example MHOs involved in mental health law, and how they should give effect to the principles of the Act. It also set out the circumstances in which a person with mental disorder may receive treatment and/or be detained on a compulsory basis, and the procedures which have to be followed including the additional rights the Act gives to a person with mental disorder associated safeguards.

Principles developed by the Millan Committee informed the Scottish Executive's thinking when developing the policy for the 2003 Act. These principles are laid out in Box 34.

Box 34   The Millan principles

Principle	Explanation
Non-Discrimination	People with mental disorder should wherever possible retain the same rights and entitlements as those with other health needs.
Equality	All powers under the Act should be exercised without any direct or indirect discrimination on the grounds of physical disability, age, gender, sexual orientation, language, religion or national, ethnic, or social origin.
Respect for Diversity	Service users should receive care treatment and support in a manner that accords respect for their individual qualities, abilities and diverse background and properly takes into account their age, gender, sexual orientation, ethnic group, social, cultural and religious background.
Reciprocity	Where society imposes an obligation on an individual to comply with a programme of treatment of care, it should impose a parallel obligation on the health and social care authorities to provide safe and appropriate services, including ongoing care following discharge from compulsion.
Informal Care	Wherever possible care, treatment and support should be provided to people with mental disorders without the use of compulsory powers.
Participation	Service users should be fully involved so far as they are able to be in all aspects of their assessment, care, treatment and support. Their past and present wishes should be taken into account. Due consideration should be given to an advanced statement. They should be provided with all information and support necessary to enable them to participate fully. Information should be provided in a way which makes it most likely to be understood.
Respect for Carers	Those who provide care to service users on an informal basis should receive respect for their role and experience, receive appropriate information and advice and have their views and needs taken into account.
Least Restrictive Alternative	Service users should be provided with any necessary care, treatment and support both in the least invasive manner and the least restrictive manner and environment compatible with the delivery of safe and effective care, taking account where appropriate of the safety of others.
Benefit	Any intervention under the Act should be likely to produce for the service user a benefit that cannot reasonably be achieved other than by intervention.
Child Welfare	The welfare of a child with mental disorder should be paramount in any interventions imposed on the child under the Act.

(NHS Education for Scotland, 2005)

Though the Millan principles inform the legislation, sections 1–3 of the Mental Health (Care and Treatment) (Scotland) Act 2003 give statutory effect to some of them, as outlined in Box 35.

Box 35   Mental Health (Care and Treatment) (Scotland) Act 2003 principles

Professionals exercising their powers under this act are required to have regard to the following matters:

- the present and past wishes and feelings of the patient
- the views of:

    - the patient's named person

    - any carer of the patient

    - any guardian of the patient

    - any welfare attorney of the patient

- the importance of the patient participating as fully as possible
- the importance of providing such information and support to the patient as is necessary to enable the patient to participate
- the range of options available in the patient's case
- the importance of providing the maximum benefit to the patient
- the need to ensure that, unless it can be shown that it is justified in the circumstances, the patient is not treated in a way that is less favourable than the way in which a person who is not a patient might be treated in a comparable situation
- the patient's abilities, background and characteristics, including, without prejudice to that generality, the patient's age, sex, sexual orientation, religious persuasion, racial origin, cultural and linguistic background and membership of any ethnic group.

The principle of minimum intervention also applies.

The welfare of a patient who is a child is paramount.

There is substantial overlap between the Millan principles and those contained in Part 1 of the Mental Health (Care and Treatment) (Scotland) Act 2003. For example, as you can see from the above lists both sets of principles refer to the need to take into account the 'present and past wishes and feelings' of service users (the term 'patient' is used in the Act) as well as the service user's 'age, gender, sexual orientation', religious persuasion, racial origin, cultural and linguistic background. The Act refers to 'the importance of providing maximum benefit to the patient' – in the language of the Millan principles any intervention should be 'likely to produce for the service user a benefit that cannot reasonably be achieved other than by intervention'. These principles are central to the Act in that they should determine the way in which service users experience professional intervention under the Act and shape how they are approached by mental health professionals.

Before looking at the Mental Health (Care and Treatment) (Scotland) Act 2003 in more detail it is important to note briefly the roles and responsibilities of key people (including mental health professionals) and institutions under the legislation. The main ones are described in Box 36.

Box 36   Mental Health (Care and Treatment) (Scotland) Act 2003 – roles and responsibilities

Personnel

Mental health officer (MHO)

The MHO is an 'officer of the local authority' who must be qualified as a social worker. An MHO will have had appropriate training and will have experience of dealing with people with mental health problems. They will be independent. They have duties and powers in relation to the compulsory admission and detention of people in hospital and those on a guardianship order in the community.

Responsible medical officer (RMO)

Every patient who is compulsorily admitted to hospital is allocated a responsible medical officer (RMO), a doctor on the staff of the hospital who has responsibility for that particular patient.

Approved Medical Practitioner (AMP)

An AMP is specialist medical practitioner, with experience of diagnosing and treating mental disorders, named on a list maintained by a health board

Named person

Service users aged 16 or over will be able to choose someone, a 'named person', to support them and to protect their interests in any proceedings under the Act. The named person will have the same rights as the service user to be notified of, attend and be represented at tribunal hearings. If no one is chosen by the service user, then the 'primary carer' will be the named person (this is the carer who provides most or all of the person's care and support). If there is no primary carer, then the service user's nearest relative will be the named person

Institutions

Mental Welfare Commission

The task of the MWC is to protect mentally disordered people who cannot protect themselves or their interests. The MWC's remit covers patients who are detained as well as those who are in hospital voluntarily and those who are in the community. It publishes annual reports in which it is often critical of practices in relation to the care of the mentally disordered. It investigates complaints, plays an important role where a second opinion is required before treatment can be given without a patient's consent, and regularly visits all patients who are compulsorily detained in hospital or who are on a guardianship order. The MWC also has duties to investigate concerns about the personal welfare of an adult under the Adults With Incapacity (Scotland) Act 2000.

Mental Health Tribunal for Scotland

The Mental Health Tribunal for Scotland is a new, independent judicial body. It makes decisions on the care and treatment of patients who are subject to the Act.

The tribunal has three groups of members: legal, medical, and general. Each hearing will have a panel of three members that includes one person from each group. The legal members will chair the hearing. Medical members are psychiatrists. General members are people with a special interest in mental health including psychiatric nurses, social workers, psychologists, service users and carers. Proceedings are heard in private, usually in the hospital where the patient is subject to the Act as an in-patient.

The types of proceedings that the tribunal will deal with are:
- applications to the tribunal, e.g. compulsory treatment orders (CTO)
- references to the tribunal, e.g. from the commission
- appeals to the tribunal from patients or named persons
- reviews by the tribunal.

There is one further aspect of the Mental Health (Care and Treatment) (Scotland) Act 2003 that it is important to note at this stage: advance statements. The Act gives recognition to advance statements about treatment for a mental disorder. This statement must be in writing and must be witnessed. When a person comes under compulsion, a doctor treating that person must have regard to the advance statement and if the doctor decides to treat the patient against the wishes expressed in the statement that must be reported to the MWC. Advance statements are an integral part of the Act's concern to recognise the rights and interests of mental health service users.

Activity 23 provides an opportunity to acquire an overview of the key features of emergency and short-term detention under the Act.

Allow about 1 hour

Activity 23   Understanding mental health law

Website

Following the link from this activity on the course website, look at the Law Resource and make notes on the following questions:

1   What is meant by the term 'mental disorder'?

2   What are the grounds for an emergency detention certificate?

3   What are the key differences between an emergency detention certificate and a short-term detention certificate?

Comment

The term 'mental disorder' is a key concept in the application of the Mental Health (Care and Treatment) (Scotland) Act 2003. Before someone can be compulsorily detained in hospital, they have to be diagnosed as suffering from a mental disorder. However, there is some difficulty in deciding exactly what this definition covers. It includes mental illness, personality disorder and learning disability 'however caused or manifested'. Mental illness would include such disorders as dementia, schizophrenia and depression. However, there can be disagreements about what constitutes a mental

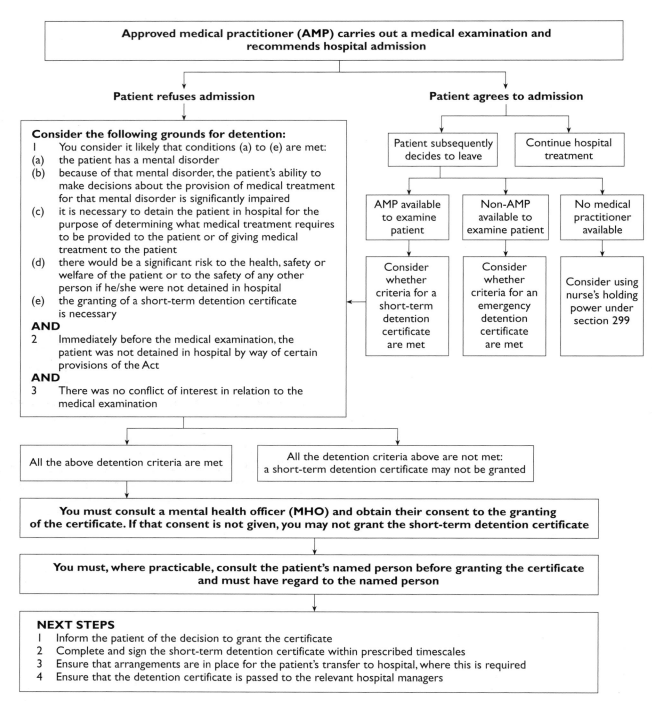

Figure 2   The processes and personnel involved in making a short-term detention certificate

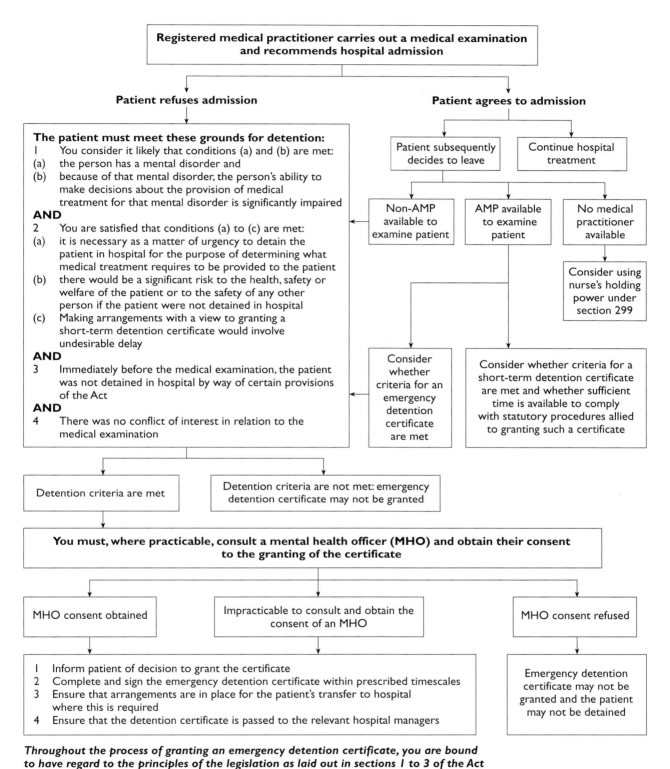

Registered medical practitioner carries out a medical examination and recommends hospital admission

Patient refuses admission

The patient must meet these grounds for detention:

1   You consider it likely that conditions (a) and (b) are met:
(a) the person has a mental disorder and
(b) because of that mental disorder, the person's ability to make decisions about the provision of medical treatment for that mental disorder is significantly impaired

AND

2   You are satisfied that conditions (a) to (c) are met:
(a) it is necessary as a matter of urgency to detain the patient in hospital for the purpose of determining what medical treatment requires to be provided to the patient
(b) there would be a significant risk to the health, safety or welfare of the patient or to the safety of any other person if the patient were not detained in hospital
(c) Making arrangements with a view to granting a short-term detention certificate would involve undesirable delay

AND

3   Immediately before the medical examination, the patient was not detained in hospital by way of certain provisions of the Act

AND

4   There was no conflict of interest in relation to the medical examination

Patient agrees to admission

Patient subsequently decides to leave

Continue hospital treatment

Non-AMP available to examine patient

AMP available to examine patient

No medical practitioner available

Consider using nurse's holding power under section 299

Consider whether criteria for an emergency detention certificate are met

Consider whether criteria for a short-term detention certificate are met and whether sufficient time is available to comply with statutory procedures allied to granting such a certificate

Detention criteria are met

Detention criteria are not met: emergency detention certificate may not be granted

You must, where practicable, consult a mental health officer (MHO) and obtain their consent to the granting of the certificate

MHO consent obtained

Impracticable to consult and obtain the consent of an MHO

MHO consent refused

1   Inform patient of decision to grant the certificate
2   Complete and sign the emergency detention certificate within prescribed timescales
3   Ensure that arrangements are in place for the patient's transfer to hospital where this is required
4   Ensure that the detention certificate is passed to the relevant hospital managers

Emergency detention certificate may not be granted and the patient may not be detained

Throughout the process of granting an emergency detention certificate, you are bound to have regard to the principles of the legislation as laid out in sections 1 to 3 of the Act

Figure 3   The processes and personnel involved in making an emergency detention certificate

illness: for example, should someone with an eating disorder be regarded as suffering from a mental disorder and therefore liable to be treated or detained under the Mental Health (Care and Treatment) (Scotland) Act 2003?

While there are some similarities between the grounds for emergency detention certificates and short-term detention certificates there are some important differences. Emergency detention is for assessment only and no treatment can be given under an emergency detention certificate. Another difference is that an AMP must recommend hospital admission in relation to short-term detention while the recommendation of a GP is sufficient for an emergency detention certificate. Another key difference relates to the role of the MHO. In relation to a short-term detention certificate the AMP must consult with a MHO and get their consent to the granting of a short term detention certificate whereas in relation to an emergency detention order the GP should consult with a MHO and obtain their consent though need not do so if it is not practicable. Figures 2 and 3 outline the key processes and personnel involved in the making of short-term detention and emergency detention certificates.

A number of requirements have to be met before someone can be made subject to a short-term detention certificate under section 44 of the Mental Health (Care and Treatment) (Scotland) Act 2003, as set out in Box 37. In addition, the human rights dimension must be taken into account. Compulsory admission is a deprivation of liberty under Article 5 of the European Convention on Human Rights (ECHR). However, Article 5 does permit restriction of liberty for 'persons of unsound mind', as long as it is done lawfully. The Mental Health (Care and Treatment) (Scotland) Act 2003 should be compatible with the ECHR, since the Scottish Parliament is not permitted to pass legislation that does not comply with the ECHR, but the provisions of the Act must be strictly adhered to, ensuring that there is an objective assessment of a mental disorder which warrants detention and that detention lasts no longer than is necessary.

Box 37   Requirements for short-term detention

An approved medical practitioner must certify that:

- the patient has a mental disorder
- because of the mental disorder, the patient's ability to make decisions about the provision of medical treatment is significantly impaired
- it is necessary to detain the patient in hospital for the purpose of determining what medical treatment should be given to the patient, or giving medical treatment to the patient
- if the patient were not detained in hospital there would be a significant risk to the health, safety or welfare of the patient, or to the safety of any other person
- the granting of a short-term detention certificate is necessary.

The AMP must obtain the consent of a mental health officer.

(Scottish Executive, 2005c)

Activity 24 allows you to consider the principles contained in the Mental Health (Care and Treatment) (Scotland) Act 2003 and the basis on which a patient can be compelled to have treatment.

Allow about 1 hour

Website

Activity 24   Taking compulsory measures

Read the following case study.

> Mr Blair, who is aged 45, has been acting strangely for some time. One of his neighbours has phoned the local GP's surgery to say that Mr Blair seems to have barricaded himself in his house. He has appeared at the window from time to time. He looks unkempt and is shouting and swearing and issuing threats. He seems to think that someone is trying to 'get him'. The shouting has continued during the night and some of the residents are becoming alarmed.
>
> Mr Blair has spent periods in hospital in the past and has been diagnosed with schizophrenia. Paul Green, the MHO who has been working with Mr Blair, cannot gain entry to the house. Mr Blair has no insight into the fact that he is ill and will not cooperate with the doctor in agreeing to go into hospital. Mr Blair has one sister, Alice, who lives 30 miles away. She rarely sees him because she finds his behaviour frightening.

Following the link from this activity on the course website, read the Law Resource and then:

1   Identify what you think are the relevant principles of the Mental Health (Care and Treatment) (Scotland) Act 2003 that should apply here.

2   Outline the options available for securing treatment for Mr Blair.

Comment

The relevant principles would include the requirement to have regard to the 'present and past wishes and feelings' of Mr Blair, the importance of Mr Blair 'participating as fully as possible' and 'the importance of providing the maximum benefit' to Mr Blair. Depending on how the situation develops other principles might assume greater significance, for example the least restrictive intervention principle.

At a practical level as the MHO cannot initially gain access to the premises where Mr Blair is living and if he is unable to persuade Mr Blair to allow him to enter his house, under section 35 of the Mental Health (Care and Treatment) (Scotland) Act 2003 he could apply to a sheriff or justice of the peace for a warrant authorising him to enter the premises, accompanied by the police, and to medically examine Mr Blair in the event of his refusal. In addition he could apply for a warrant to remove Mr Blair to a place of safety (the local psychiatric unit or hospital) under section 293 of the Mental Health (Care and Treatment) (Scotland) Act 2003.

In terms of section 36 of the Mental Health (Care and Treatment) (Scotland) Act 2003 the GP could recommend that Mr Blair be admitted to hospital for up to 72 hours if it is not practicable to use the short-term detention process. The GP should ask Paul Green as MHO, to give his consent to the admission. Any treatment proposed within the 72-hour period can only take place with the patient's consent, although doctors have a common law power to intervene if it is necessary in the interests of the patient.

Should Mr Blair's condition not respond to treatment within the 72-hour period, and he continues to require treatment and is a risk either to himself or to others, he can be further detained under section 44 for up to 28 days. Mr Blair does not have any right of appeal against the section 36 order, but he can appeal against section 44. This appeal is to the mental health tribunal. In both instances he can approach the MWC to look into his case.

During the time when Mr Blair is being detained under section 44, arrangements may be made to make an application to the mental health tribunal under section 57 for a compulsory treatment order (CTO). Paul Green will be required to make this application. A section 57 application must be accompanied by two medical recommendations and a report from the MHO, which must include a care plan. If two doctors who are making the medical recommendation request the MHO to make an application to the tribunal, then the MHO cannot refuse even if he or she disagrees with the decision (s. 57 (1)).

Box 38   Compulsory treatment orders

CTOs deal with the longer-term treatment of a mental disorder. They may authorise detention in hospital, but also allow for treatment and supervision in the community. The 2003 Act presumes that treatment will take place in the community, unless that is not appropriate. The tribunal may attach conditions to the order to ensure that it meets the needs of the individual for whom it is sought. The order may be terminated if the RMO or the MWC considers that it is no longer required (for example, if the patient is cooperating with the treatment regime and care plan). Where a CTO requires a patient to accept compulsion in the community, there is clearly a need to have the cooperation of the patient and his or her carers to make it a viable option. A multidisciplinary approach to care and treatment is also an essential component.

Figure 4 outlines the key processes and personnel involved in the making of a compulsory treatment order.

The task of Paul Green acting as MHO is to satisfy himself that a CTO is, in all the circumstances of the case, the most appropriate way of providing the care and medical treatment that the patient needs The ways in which he would ensure that it is appropriate for Mr Blair to be detained in hospital would be to:

- assess Mr Blair's mental state and from this gauge his need for support and treatment
- assess Mr Blair's preparedness to stay in hospital on a voluntary basis
- assess the feasibility of alternatives to hospital care
- look into his social circumstances, which would include discussions with Alice
- identify potential resources that could inform treatment and discharge decisions
- produce a draft care plan to accompany the application.

Mr Blair, his representative, his named person and any independent advocate would have the opportunity to appear at this hearing before the tribunal, but if the application is granted there is no right of appeal. The CTO lasts for six months and it can be renewed after this period. He can appeal against the renewal and, of course, he can approach the MWC at any time to look into his case. Throughout, the RMO has a duty to discharge Mr Blair if the grounds for the CTO cease to exist.

Paul Green will plan how his needs may best be served in the community both during the CTO and afterwards and this may entail arranging some form of supported accommodation for him. Paul Green would also provide follow-up support. Conditions can be attached to CTOs (see Box 39).

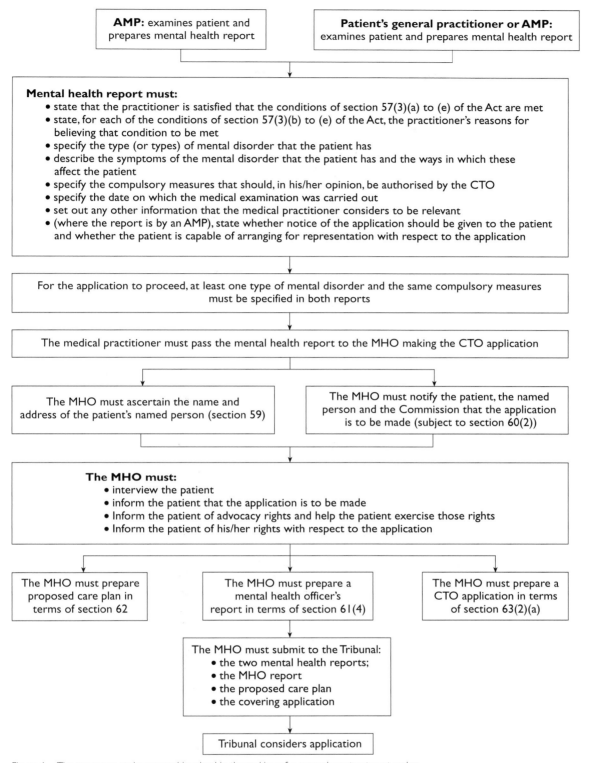

Figure 4   The processes and personnel involved in the making of a compulsory treatment order

Box 39   Conditions that can be attached to CTOs

- That you have to stay in hospital
- That you may be given medical treatment under the rules set out in Part 16 of the Mental Health (Care and Treatment) (Scotland) Act 2003
- That you have to attend for medical treatment as instructed
- That you have to attend certain community care services
- That you have to stay at a particular place in the community

> - That you have to allow visits in your home by people involved in your care and treatment
> - That you have to notify your MHO if you want to change your address
> - That your MHO has to agree to any change in your address
>
> These conditions can be changed during the course of the CTO. So, for example, you could start out on a hospital-based order, and this could be changed to a community-based order. If the doctor in charge of your care wants to change the conditions, he/she has to follow procedures set out in the Act. This involves him/her making an application to the Tribunal. You, and your named person, would be told about this, and would have a chance to give your views before the Tribunal makes a decision.
>
> (Scottish Executive, 2005c, p. 4)

The remainder of this section will consider some aspects of the role of the MHO under the Mental Health (Care and Treatment) (Scotland) Act 2003 and the Adults With Incapacity (Scotland) Act 2000 and the rights of service users

4.3 The role of the mental health officer

The local authority has a duty to provide or secure provision of social care and support services for persons who have or who have had a mental disorder and are not in hospital. Such care and support services include residential accommodation and personal care and personal support, but not nursing care. Section 32 of the Act requires a local authority to appoint a sufficient number of persons to discharge in their area the functions of MHOs and section 229 requires local authorities to appoint an MHO after a 'relevant event' (under section 232 defined as the granting of a short-term detention certificate or the making of a range of compulsory orders, for example a CTO). To be appointed as an MHO, a qualified social worker must have a minimum of two years post-qualifying experience and have completed a specified amount of specialised training. Social workers seeking to be appointed as MHOs must therefore undergo an approved MHO training course in addition to having the necessary registration and qualifying experience before they can be appointed as an MHO by a local authority.

The role of a MHO includes interviewing service users, advising them of their rights, for example to independent advocacy, to have a named person look after their interests and, as noted in Activity 24, applying for a CTO.

Table 4 summarises the legal mandate for the role of the MHO under the Mental Health (Care and Treatment) (Scotland) Act 2003.

Table 4 The role of the mental health officer

Section	Legal requirements	MHO role
Section 36 Emergency recommendation. Max. period of detention: 72 hours. Only to be used if short-term detention procedure would involve undesirable delay.	Recommendation by medical practitioner following personal examination of individual. 'Where practicable' consent of an MHO obtained.	The MHO has to satisfy themselves that admission to hospital is, in all circumstances of the case, the most appropriate way of providing the care and medical treatment the patient needs. To do this the MHO: • interviews the individual to assess the potential risks to self or others • attempts to advise the individual of their rights, including the right to an independent advocate • interviews medical and nursing staff • contacts the police if they are involved and still present • consults medical or social work records On the basis of all the evidence the MHO will consider possible alternatives to admission to hospital. On the basis of all the evidence the MHO either gives or withholds their consent. The MHO also speaks to the named person after the decision is made to explain the situation and explain their own rights.
Section 36 Emergency recommendation in respect of a patient already in hospital. Max. period of detention: 72 hours or 2 hours by a qualified nurse if a doctor is not immediately available.	As above.	A hospital-based MHO may have already been involved in discussion with medical staff before the process is set in motion.
Section 44 Short-term detention. Max. period of detention: 28 days.	Approved medical practitioner to certify the grounds mentioned above. Consent to the short-term detention certificate must be obtained from an MHO.	As for section 36. Process will involve the MHO interviewing the individual, their named person, medical and nursing staff, consulting records etc. The report may include the MHO's opinion as to whether or not they felt admission to hospital was justified. They may also include information on possible future social support needs.

Section 57 Application for CTO (may follow on from short-term detention or apply to someone living in the community or in hospital moving out to the community on a CTO). Max. period of compulsion: 6 months (at the end of period application for renewal can be made).	Application for order made to the mental health tribunal by an MHO. Application to be founded on and accompanied by two medical recommendations, including a statement of the form of mental disorder and a statement of the grounds for a CTO.	Same core tasks as for sections 36 and 44. These include interviewing the individual both to assess the risks posed and to advise them of their right to contest the application, their right to an independent advocate and to be legally represented. Some MHOs may also obtain a solicitor on the person's behalf. MHOs will speak to members of the individual's social network before making the application, both to obtain information and to advise them of the proposed application and their own rights to appeal against detention. Drawing all the material together the MHO's application will include a statement as to whether or not the application should be granted and stating the grounds for this opinion. If the application is contested the MHO will appear as a witness at the tribunal.
Section 25	The local authority shall provide care and support services for anyone who is or has been suffering from mental disorder. (These services are part of 'community care services'.)	MHOs may plan, coordinate and provide social work follow-up support, as appropriate, within the constraints of their workload and social work team policy; or contact may end when legal duties are complete.
Section 26	The local authority shall provide services designed to promote well-being and social development for anyone who is or has been suffering from mental disorder.	
Section 27	The local authority shall provide assistance with travel for anyone who is or has been suffering from mental disorder.	

In addition, the MHO has duties under the Adults With Incapacity (Scotland) Act 2000, as outlined in Box 40.

Box 40 MHO duties under the Adults With Incapacity (Scotland) Act 2000

- To investigate circumstances where the personal welfare of an adult with incapacity is at risk
- To supervise welfare attorneys and guardians
- To provide a report to the sheriff in relation to applications for welfare intervention or welfare guardianship.

Obviously, when some patients are acutely ill they can be totally unaware of the extent of their disturbance and refuse medication. The Mental Health (Care and Treatment) (Scotland) Act 2003 allows treatment for a patient's mental disorder without consent except in the 72-hour period of an emergency admission under section 36. A patient who is detained in hospital under sections 44 or 57 can be given medical treatment for their mental disorder for up to two months without their consent. After the two-month period the patient must either give consent or a second opinion must be obtained from a doctor appointed by the MWC, defined as a designated medical practitioner (DMP). If the doctor attending Mr Blair (see Activity 24) decided that he required ECT, he or she would need to get Mr Blair's consent since it cannot be given without consent to a competent patient. If Mr Blair is incapable of consenting, ECT can be authorised by a second doctor. Psychosurgery or surgical implants to reduce sex drive can only proceed with consent and a second opinion.

Guardianship is available under the Adults With Incapacity (Scotland) Act 2000 for persons with incapacity and can be used in a number of ways. It can be used as a long-term plan to sustain and support individuals in the community; as a way of trying to provide people with some supervision and secure their continued cooperation with treatment; and as a short-term strategy to transfer people from their homes or hospital into nursing or residential care.

Allow about 40 minutes

Activity 25 Guardianship

Read the following case study and make notes on the issues which it raises

> Robbie Scott is a 64-year-old man with a history of bipolar disorder (manic depression). He has been known to the social work department for a number of years and has recently been diagnosed with Alzheimer's. He lives alone in a tenement flat. Ann Bell, his MHO, took a lot of trouble to get him this flat because when Robbie first came to her attention he was living rough. However, Ann has concerns about his deteriorating condition and is concerned that he will fail to attend for outpatient treatment for his depression. She fears the possible deterioration of his mental health and quality of life as a consequence.

Comment

Ann is facing the kind of social work dilemma you have considered before. She wants to maintain Robbie's right to self-determination but she does not wish to see his health suffer to such a degree that a compulsory admission to hospital for further treatment might be necessary. The law recognises this dilemma and offers Ann a possible solution – guardianship. It is an alternative to compulsory hospitalisation that gives the guardian some powers.

In relation to Robbie, and any person for whom guardianship is considered, there are some questions that need to be asked in deciding whether guardianship is a suitable option:

- Is the adult incapable in relation to making decisions about or of acting to promote or safeguard his interests in his property, financial affairs or personal welfare?

- Are there any other means available under the Act to safeguard or promote the adult's interests?

If the answer to these questions is 'yes', then an application can be made to the sheriff.

Ann would probably want to insist that Robbie attends his outpatient appointments. She might also want him to stay living where he is and not return to living rough. Prior to April 2002 there were limitations to the effectiveness of a guardianship order in that it could not be tailored to meet the needs of the individual and the guardian could not deal with property nor take medical decisions for the individual concerned. For guardians appointed since April 2002, or those who have applied to have their powers changed, some of these issues can now be addressed. However, a guardian cannot override a competent refusal to take medical treatment and it will not always be the case that an incapable adult is incompetent to take all medical decisions for themselves.

There are some important differences in powers of intervention between the Adults With Incapacity (Scotland) Act 2000 and the Mental Health (Care and Treatment) (Scotland) Act 2003. Box 41 outlines the relationship between the Adults With Incapacity (Scotland) Act 2000 and the Mental Health (Care and Treatment) (Scotland) Act 2003 in relation to medical treatment.

Box 41   Medical treatment: the relationship between the Adults With Incapacity (Scotland) Act 2000 and the Mental Health (Care and Treatment) (Scotland) Act 2003

The Adults With Incapacity (Scotland) Act 2000 provides a general authority for the medical treatment of adults who lack the ability to make medical decisions for themselves, due to mental incapacity, or severe communication difficulties caused by a physical disorder.

Section 47 of the Adults With Incapacity (Scotland) Act 2000 allows the medical practitioner to complete a certificate certifying that in their opinion the adult is incapable of making a decision on the medical treatment in question. The authority to grant a certificate under section 47(1) was extended in 2005 to health professionals who have relevant qualifications and training to assess incapacity – these are registered nurses, dentists and ophthalmic opticians – though this is limited to the issue of certificates within their own area of competence.

Where the medical practitioner complies with the certification requirements set out in section 47 of that Act and completes a treatment plan, they then have authority to give what treatment is reasonable in the circumstances provided the intervention represents the least restrictive method and that the treatments involved are the minimum necessary interventions to safeguard or promote the physical or mental health of the adult.

Although the guardian or attorney cannot authorise the admission of a patient to a mental hospital for treatment, there may be patients for whom community-based treatment under the Adults With Incapacity (Scotland) Act 2000 would be appropriate. Therefore the Adults With Incapacity (Scotland) Act 2000 could be used as an alternative to the Mental Health (Care and Treatment) (Scotland) Act 2003 for some patients. However, compulsory treatment in the community against a person's will cannot be administered under the Adults With Incapacity (Scotland) Act 2000

4.4 Service user rights

Activity 26 provides you with an opportunity to clarify the law on consent to medical treatment, named persons and advance statements which was discussed briefly earlier in this section. Boxes 42 and 43 are important resources for this activity.

Box 42   Advance statements

The Act allows a patient to make an advance statement. This is a written statement setting out how they would wish to be treated, or wish not to be treated, for mental disorder should their ability to make decisions about treatment for their mental disorder become significantly impaired as a result of their mental disorder. An advance statement might also contain information concerning early changes in symptoms, thinking and behaviour. This information might facilitate interventions aimed at preventing the need for treatment under compulsion. Doctors discharging functions under the Act *must* have regard to an advance statement.

When someone assists a patient in producing an advance statement, it is good practice to ensure that the statement reflects the patient's wishes, that the patient understands that a medical practitioner must have regard for the statement and the process by which a medical practitioner might act against the stated wishes and the actions to be taken in such circumstances.

An advance statement must be in writing, signed and dated by the patient and witnessed by a *prescribed person*. It should ideally contain the name and address of the patient, the witness, and the patient's GP, and details of any named person or carer.

A doctor intending to provide medical treatment should ask the patient if they have an advance statement and where it is stored, and explain that they wish to see it before making their decision regarding medical treatment. Ideally the patient's general practitioner, responsible medical officer, named person, primary carer, independent advocate and mental health officer should all have a copy of the current advance statement.

If a doctor makes a decision or authorises treatment under the Act which conflicts with the wishes specified in the advance statement, the Act requires that the doctor record in writing the reasons for this decision. The Act requires that a copy of this record is sent to:

- the patient who has made the advance statement;
- the patient's named person;
- any guardian or welfare attorney of the patient;
- the Mental Welfare Commission; and
- patient's medical records.

A competently made advance statement should be a strong indication of a patient's wishes about medical treatment but should not be considered in isolation from the surrounding circumstances.

(NHS Education for Scotland, 2005)

Box 43   Named persons

The role of the named person is to represent and safeguard the interests of the patient. The named person and the patient are entitled to act independently of each other. For instance, a named person can apply to the Tribunal for a review of the patient's compulsory treatment order with or without the patient's approval. The named person has the right to put his or her own view forward, even when the patient has a different view.

The Act requires any person exercising functions under the Act to take account of the views of the named person when making a decision or considering a course of action, where it is reasonable and practicable to do so.

A patient aged 16 or over may choose an individual who agrees to be their named person. In the absence of a patient nominating a named person then their primary carer or nearest relative will be the named person. An MHO can apply to the Tribunal if they believe a named person is unsuitable for the role. The Tribunal also has the power to make an order declaring that the acting named person is not the named person or specifying someone else to be the named person in that person's place.

The named person must have attained at least 16 years of age. The named person should not be someone with a professional relationship with the patient, such as a doctor or anyone who works to deliver care or treatment to the patient, as it could create a conflict of interest.

The nomination may be made whether or not the patient is, at the time, the subject of compulsory measures under the 2003 Act. The patient must have the capacity to understand the decision they are making and its effects, and have not been subject to any undue influence.

(NHS Education for Scotland, 2005)

Allow about 30 minutes

Website

Activity 26   Consent to treatment, named persons and advance statements

Following the link from this activity on the course website, look at the Law Resource about named persons. Read Boxes 42 and 43 and then make notes on the following questions:

1   Who can choose a named person and what are the consequences of not nominating a named person?

2   What are the powers of a named person?

3   What is an advance statement and why is it so important?

Comment

A person aged 16 or over can nominate a named person; they do not have to do so but one consequence of not doing so will be that the service user's primary carer will be asked to assume the role and if the primary carer is not available then the 'nearest relative'. The advance statement is important precisely because it must be taken into account when decisions are being taken about medical care and treatment. If the medical care and treatment given departs from the advance statement the service user must be given a reason and a copy of these reasons must be given to the service user's named person, and the Mental Welfare Commission.

The advance statement can indicate both what treatment the service user would like as well as treatment they do not want to receive, for example that they would prefer individual therapy to group therapy or their wishes regarding medication and particular treatments like ECT.

Activity 26 illustrates the way in which the Mental Health (Care and Treatment) (Scotland) Act 2003 has attempted to facilitate the voice of mental health service users in particular sets of circumstances. Activity 27, through directly hearing the voices of mental health service users, allows you to explore in more detail just why it is so important to involve and engage people who use mental health services.

Allow about 45 minutes

Activity 27   Mental health service users

Audio CD

Listen to the interview with two users of mental health services from the Highlands User Group and make notes on the following questions:

1   What for you were the key lessons for professionals as the users of mental health services discussed their experiences?

2   Why was the social work support experienced by one of the service users so important?

3   In what ways has the Mental Health (Care and Treatment) (Scotland) Act 2003 improved the situation for users of mental health services?

4   Why is the service user input on the mental health tribunal so important?

Comment

Mental health service users face a number of challenges both in relation to accepting and managing their mental health needs and in their possible encounters with the use of compulsory powers.

Debbie referred to feelings of powerlessness and a sense of being threatened by the power of health professionals. Fiona talked of the newness of having contact for the first time with health professionals and being made aware of 'what health professionals can do to you'. Continuity of care, practical support for managing her own mental ill-health and support for her family were some of the positive benefits that came out of having the same social worker for seven years. The Mental Health (Care and Treatment) (Scotland) Act 2003 has improved the situation facing service users through a number of important reforms, including the introduction of advance statements, the provisions relating to named persons and the setting up of mental health tribunals. The service user input on mental health tribunals is important because it allows the tribunal to properly consider the service user experience and their care needs as well as ensuring that the tribunal operates in an open and fair manner.

4.5 Conclusion

You have looked at the legal and social work practice issues raised by working with people with mental health needs. The work of the MHO is very demanding and complex. Other individuals such as the named person, the RMO and bodies such as the MWC, also play important roles in the system. The new Act will make many changes to the system over the next few years and should lead to a different sort of approach with the move away from the presumption of detention in hospital and a move towards giving patients more say in how they are treated. This area of social work raises issues of conflicting rights and demands, since social workers are required to encourage service users to take more control of their lives, but at the same time, must protect service users and others who may be at risk. It also raises human rights issues, since Article 5 gives a right to liberty and security of person.

Key points

- The MHO is an independent professional who plays a key role in work with people with mental health problems.
- The principles contained in sections 1–3 of the Mental Health (Care and Treatment) (Scotland) Act 2003 are central to good practice.
- The participation of service users and involvement of carers is required by the Mental Health (Care and Treatment) (Scotland) Act 2003.
- The five principles of the Adults With Incapacity (Scotland) Act 2000 are fundamental to the effective operation of the Act.
- The law allows for the compulsory treatment of those suffering from a mental disorder.
- A person suffering from a mental disorder can only be compulsorily admitted to hospital if the disorder is susceptible to treatment.
- A CTO is intended to ensure that the patient with long-term mental health problems receives treatment and care in the community.
- The Mental Health Tribunal for Scotland is an important safeguard of service users' and carers' rights.
- The role of the MWC is to protect those suffering from a mental disorder; it includes the power to conduct investigations and to discharge patients.
- The vast majority of admissions to hospital are voluntary.

Allow about 1 hour   ## 4.6 Consolidation activity

Read the following case and make notes on the questions that follow.

Ms Elizabeth Brown (78) lives in sheltered accommodation with her brother Mr Alan Brown (82). They have shared this flat for the past 10 years following the death of their mother (then aged 95 years) and the sale of the family home. Both Mr and Ms Brown had led busy professional lives until their retirement, when Ms Brown took over the care of their then increasingly frail mother. Ms Brown has continued to care for her brother since their mother's death and they are described by neighbours as being 'inseparable'. Neither had ever married and they have been separated only by Mr Brown's war service during World War II. Their nearest relative is a niece, Lucy (43), the daughter of their deceased younger sister.

Ms Brown has recently been admitted to hospital following a fall at home. She has broken a hip but is recovering well from the injury. However, medical staff are concerned that her fall may have been caused by her having had a slight stroke. She now suffers from intermittent bouts of memory loss and confusion. She is, however, adamant that she wishes to return home, although her brother is not sure that he can cope.

As a social worker in the hospital, you are approached by Lucy and asked to find a nursing home place for her aunt.

1   How would you respond?

2   What do you think would be the issues of greatest concern in this case?

3   What risks, needs and rights are involved?

4   What is the legal context?

Comment

Any holistic assessment of Ms Brown's needs must take account of her being part of a family, the other members of which have their own needs. This may lead to a complex set of competing demands and it is important for the social worker to retain a sense of focus.

The main issues include Ms Brown's deteriorating physical and mental health, Mr Brown's ability to cope with his sister's care needs and the extent to which their niece is expected to provide care. Much of the information about these issues would be contained in the needs assessment you undertake in respect of Ms Brown: any assessment of her needs would have to take account of the needs of her carers.

You would wish to consider the balance to be struck between Ms Brown's right to return to her own home and the risks this may involve for Mr Brown in terms of his own health and ability to cope with the demands likely to be placed on him should Ms Brown's wish to return home be granted. Their niece must also be considered, as she, too, has a right to be consulted about future plans – particularly as they affect her ability to continue to offer care and support to her relatives. As has been stated earlier, the balance between ensuring appropriate care is provided and allowing adults to make decisions about their lives is at times a difficult one to get right.

Discussing the needs assessment would include an exploration of the duties and powers available under the full range of community care legislation as it affects all three family members, including:

- the duty to provide a community care assessment for Ms Brown under section 12A Social Work (Scotland) Act 1968

- the duty to offer aids and adaptations to the family home using the Chronically Sick and Disabled Persons Act 1970

- the duty to take account of Mr Brown's needs as a carer under section 12AA of the Social Work (Scotland) Act 1968.

When making any decisions about how best to use the legal framework, the social worker has a degree of discretion and choice that needs to be exercised thoughtfully.

References

Aberdeen City Council (2002) *Social Work Service Care Management Standards*, Aberdeen, Aberdeen City Council.

Age Concern (2003) *Rising to the Challenge of Improving Scotland's Health*, Age Concern Scotland, briefing paper, September.

Age Concern (2005) *How Ageist is Britain?*, London, Age Concern.

Ashton, K. and Gould, J. (1997) 'Community care: a duty to care?', *Legal Action*, May.

BBC News (2007) 'Figures for care waiting revealed' [online], http://news.bbc.co.uk/1/hi/scotland/5073964.stm (Accessed 24 January 2007).

British Medical Journal (BMJ) (2004) 'Editorial', *British Medical Journal*, vol. 329, no. 7467, pp. 634–5.

Bytheway, B. (1990) *Becoming and Being Old*, London, Sage.

Capability Scotland (2006) 'Submission by Capability Scotland' [online], http://www.scottish.parliament.uk/business/committees/health/inquiries/careInq/cfte-org-08-CapabilityScotland.htm (Accessed 8 March 2007).

Carers UK (2006) *Whose Rights Are They Anyway? Carers and the Human Rights Act*, London, Carers UK/ Calouste Gulbenkian Foundation.

Cartwright, A. (1991) 'The role of residential and nursing homes in the last year of people's lives', *British Journal of Social Work*, vol. 21, pp. 627–45.

Clackmannanshire Joint Future Management Group (2005) *Clackmannanshire Joint Future Management Group Report*, www.clacksweb.org.uk/site/documents/jointfuture/jointfuturemanagementgroupreportjune2005 (Accessed 14 March 2007).

Coulshed, V. and Orme, J. (1998) *Social Work Practice*, Basingstoke, Macmillan.

Department of Health (1989) *Caring for People: Community Care in the Next Decade and Beyond* (White Paper), Cmnd 849, London, HMSO.

Department of Health (1993) *No Longer Afraid: Safeguard of Older People in Domestic Settings*, London, HMSO.

Disability Rights Commission (DRC) (2005) *Code of Practice: The Duty to Promote Disability Equality*, [online] http://www.drc-gb.org/about_us/drc_scotland/library/publications/the_duty_to_promote_disability.aspx (Accessed 22 March 2007).

Griffiths, A., Roberts, G. and Williams, J. (1993) 'Elder abuse and the law', in Decalmer, P. and Glendinning, F. (eds) *The Mistreatment of Elderly People*, London, Sage.

Health Committee of the Scottish Parliament (2006) *Care Inquiry Report*, Edinburgh, Scottish Parliament; also available online at http://www.scottish.parliament.uk/business/committees/health/reports-06/her06-10-vol01-00.htm (Accessed 8 March 2007).

Innes, A., Blackstock, K., Mason, A., Smith, A. and Cox, S. (2005) 'Dementia care provision in rural Scotland: service users' and carers' experiences', *Health and Social Care in the Community*, vol. 13, no. 4.

Kerr, B., Gordon, J., MacDonald, C. and Stalker, K. (2005) *Effective Social Work with Older People*, Edinburgh, Scottish Executive.

Kingston, P. and Penhale, B. (1995) *Family Violence and the Caring Professions*, Basingstoke, Macmillan.

Kitwood, T. (1997) *Dementia Reconsidered: The Person Comes First*, Buckingham, Open University Press.

MacDonald, C. (2004) *Older People and Community Care in Scotland: A Review of Recent Research*, Scottish Executive Research Findings 35/2004, Edinburgh, Scottish Executive.

McKay, C. and Patrick, H. (1995) *The Care Maze: The Law and Your Rights to Community Care in Scotland*, Glasgow, ENABLE/Scottish Association for Mental Health.

McManus, J. and Thomson, L. (2005) *Mental Health and Scots Law in Practice*, Edinburgh, W. Green & Son.

Mental Welfare Commission (MWC) (2006) *Annual Report for 2005–2006*, Edinburgh, MWC.

Mental Welfare Commission for Scotland (1998) *Annual Report 1997–8*, Edinburgh, Mental Welfare Commission for Scotland.

MIND (2005) 'Statistics: how common is mental health distress?' [online], http://www.mind.org.uk/Information/Factsheets/Statistics/Statistics+1.htm#Prevalence_of_mental_health_problems_in_Great_Britain (Accessed 26 January 2007).

NHS Education for Scotland (2005) *The Mental Health (Care and Treatment) (Scotland) Act 2003: Principles of the Act* [online], http://www.nes.scot.nhs.uk/mhagp/one.htm (Accessed 17 December 2006).

Ridley, J. and Jones, L. (2002) *Direct What? A Study of Direct Payments to Mental Health Service Users*, Edinburgh, Scottish Executive.

Scottish Association for Mental Health (SAMH) (2006) *A World to Belong to Social Networks of People with Mental Health Problems*, Glasgow, SAMH.

Scottish Executive (2000a) *Joint Future Group Report*, Edinburgh, Scottish Executive.

Scottish Executive (2000b) *The Same as You? A review of services for people with Learning Disabilities*, Edinburgh, Scottish Executive.

Scottish Executive (2001a) *Guidance on Single Shared Assessment*, CCD 8/2001, Edinburgh, Health Department.

Scottish Executive (2001b) *Renewing Mental Health Law Policy Statement*, Edinburgh, Scottish Executive.

Scottish Executive (2002) *Consultation on Vulnerable Adults: Analysis of the responses* [online], http://www.scotland.gov.uk/Publications/2002/12/15871/14430 (Accessed 8 November 2006).

Scottish Executive (2005a) *Joint Future Performance Information and Assessment Framework*, Edinburgh, Scottish Executive.

Scottish Executive (2005b) *Better Outcomes for Older People*, Edinburgh, Scottish Executive; also available online at: http://www.scotland.gov.uk/Publications/2005/05/13101338/13412 (Accessed 8 November 2006).

Scottish Executive (2005c) *The New Mental Health Act: A Guide to Compulsory Treatment Orders*, Edinburgh, Scottish Executive; also available online at http://www.scotland.gov.uk/Publications/2005/12/02144025/40257#8 (Accessed 28 January 2007).

Scottish Executive (2006a) 'Greater protection for vulnerable groups' [online], news release, 26 September, http://www.scotland.gov.uk/News/Releases/2006/09/26132750 (Accessed 12 December 2006).

Scottish Executive (2006b) *Report of the 21st Century Social Work Review*, Edinburgh, Scottish Executive.

Scottish Executive Joint Future Unit (2004) *Guidance on Care Management in Community Care*, CCD 8/2004, Edinburgh, Scottish Executive; also available online at http://www.scotland.gov.uk/Resource/Doc/36496/0012581.pdf (Accessed 28 January 2007).

Scottish Home and Health Department/Scottish Health Service Planning Council (1988) *Scottish Health Authorities' Review of Priorities for the Eighties and Nineties*, Edinburgh, HMSO (SHARPEN Report).

Scottish Office (1998) *Modernising Community Care: An Action Plan*, Edinburgh, Scottish Office.

Scottish Office Social Work Services Group (1991) *Care Management and Assessment: Practitioners' Guide*, Edinburgh, HMSO.

'see me' (2005) *See Me So Far. A Review of the First 4 Years of the Scottish Anti-stigma Campaign*, Edinburgh, 'see me'; also available online at http://www.seemescotland.org.uk/about/include/downloads/14648-see_me_so_farMay06.pdf .

'see me' (2006) 'Lanarkshire hosts largest "see me" pledge signing' [online], 'see me', http://www/seemescotland.org.uk/about/news.php?id=93 (Accessed 11 December 2006).

Social Work Services Inspectorate (SWSI)/Mental Welfare Commission (MWC) (2004) *Investigations into Scottish Borders Council and NHS Borders Services for People with Learning Disabilities: Joint Statement from the Mental Welfare Commission and the Social Work Services Inspectorate*, Edinburgh, Scottish Executive.

Tatum, C. and Tucker, S. (1998) 'The concealed consequences of caring: an examination of the experiences of young carers in the community', *Youth and Policy*, no. 61, pp. 12–27.

Walker, C. and Walker, A. (1998) *Uncertain Futures: People with Learning Difficulties and their Ageing Family Carers*, Hove, Pavilion Publishing/Joseph Rowntree Foundation.

Weaver, T., Willcocks, D. and Kellaher, L. (1985) *The Business of Care: A Study of Private Residential Homes for Old People*, report no. 1, London, Polytechnic of North London Centre for Environmental and Social Studies in Ageing.

Wilkin, D. and Hughes, B. (1987) 'Residential care of elderly people: the consumers' views', *Ageing and Society*, 7, pp. 175–201.

Acknowledgements

Grateful acknowledgement is made to the following sources for permission to reproduce material within this product:

Text

Pages 14 and 15: 'Report of the Joint Future Group: Chapter 2 Recommendations and Timetable for Implementation' found at http://www.scotland.gov.uk/library3/social/rjfg-02.asp. Crown copyright material is reproduced under Class Licence Number C01W0000065 with the permission of the Controller of HMSO and the Queen's Printer for Scotland; *Pages 41 and 42*: Kerr, B., Gordon J., MacDonald C. and Stalker, K. (2005), *Effective Social Work with Older People*. Crown copyright material is reproduced under Class Licence Number C01W0000065 with the permission of the Controller of HMSO and the Queen's Printer for Scotland; *Pages 58 and 59*: 'Exercising your Rights' (Standard 10) and 'Expressing your Views' (Standard 11), in *National Care Standards: Care Homes for Older People* (2005). Crown copyright material is reproduced under Class Licence Number C01W0000065 with the permission of the Controller of HMSO and the Queen's Printer for Scotland; *Pages 68 and 69*: 'The same as you? A review of services for people with learning disabilities' found at http://www.scotland.gov.uk/Resource/Doc/159140/0043285.pdf. Crown copyright material is reproduced under Class Licence Number C01W0000065 with the permission of the Controller of HMSO and the Queen's Printer for Scotland; *Pages 98–100*: http://www.nes.scot.nhs.uk/mhagp/seven.htm. Reproduced with kind permission of NHS Education for Scotland; *Pages 98 and 99*: http://www.nes.scot.nhs.uk/mhagp/six.htm. Reproduced with kind permission of NHS Education for Scotland.

Figures

Figure 1: 'The Process of Care Management' found at http://www.scotland.gov.uk/Publications/2006/05/24093431/2. Crown copyright material is reproduced under Class Licence Number C01W0000065 with the permission of the Controller of HMSO and the Queen's Printer for Scotland; *Figure 2*: 'Guide for medical practitioners on the granting of a short-term detention certificate under section 44 of the Mental Health (Care and Treatment) (Scotland) Act 2003' in *Approved Medical Practitioners: Mental Health (Care and Treatment) (Scotland) Act, 2003 Training Manual*. Crown copyright material is reproduced under Class Licence Number C01W0000065 with the permission of the Controller of HMSO and the Queen's Printer for Scotland; *Figure 3*: 'Guide for medical practitioners on the granting of an emergency detention certificate under section 36 of the Mental Health (Care and Treatment) (Scotland) Act 2003' in *Approved Medical Practitioners: Mental Health (Care and Treatment) (Scotland) Act, 2003 Training Manual*. Crown copyright material is reproduced under Class Licence Number C01W0000065 with the permission of the Controller of HMSO and the Queen's Printer for Scotland; *Figure 4*: 'Flowchart of statutory duties to be carried out during the CTO application process (Part 7, Chapter 1)' found at http://www.nes.scot.nhs.uk/mhagp/documents/p45chart.pdf. Reprinted with permission of NHS Education for Scotland (NES).

Illustrations

Cover: © John Foxx/Getty Images; *pages 11, 29, 34, 44, 54, 64, 70 and 81*: www.johnbirdsall.co.uk